THE UTILITY
OF BOREDOM

BASEBALL ESSAYS

THE UTILITY OF BOREDOM

BASEBALL ESSAYS

Andrew Forbes

Invisible Publishing
Halifax & Toronto

Library and Archives Canada Cataloguing in Publication

Forbes, Andrew, 1976-, author
        The utility of boredom : baseball essays / Andrew Forbes.

Issued in print and electronic formats.
ISBN 978-1-926743-69-1 (paperback).--ISBN 978-1-926743-70-7 (epub).--
ISBN 978-1-926743-71-4 (mobi)

    1. Baseball. I. Title. II. Title: Baseball essays.

GV867.F67 2016   796.357   2016-900941-6
                                                 C2016-900942-4

Edited by Andrew Faulkner
Cover & Interior designed by Megan Fildes

Typeset in Laurentian and Gibson by Megan Fildes
With thanks to type designer Rod McDonald

Printed and bound in Canada

Invisible Publishing | Halifax & Toronto
www.invisiblepublishing.com

We acknowledge the support of the Canada Council for the Arts, which last year
invested $157 million to bring the arts to Canadians throughout the country.

 Canada Council   Conseil des Arts
for the Arts   du Canada

If only every day were opening day.

— Mary Schmich

Annie Savoy: Have you heard of Walt Whitman?
Ebby Calvin "Nuke" LaLoosh: No. Who's he play for?

Sportswriters, as stakeholders in the game, occupy
an interesting perch. They like to keep reminding
their audience that "baseball is a business," yet
their job is about the love of sport, and the good
ones can't help sniffing the same glue as the fans.

— Diana Goetsch

SANCTUARY

There's an old synagogue in South Bend, Indiana where they now sell baseball caps and T-shirts and foam fingers. The South Bend Cubs of the Single-A Midwest League play just across the street at Four Winds Field. The synagogue closed for worship several years ago and it proved too tempting an edifice for Andrew T. Berlin, the team's owner, to resist; he bought it and had it converted, removing the bimah and the Ark of the Covenant, installing shelving and a cash counter, and now it opens to service a different sort of adherent.

This seems entirely appropriate to me, though I understand how it might offend the Orthodox. The ballpark-as-temple notion treads the line of blasphemy, but does so acrobatically, since in the cases of both baseball and religion we're talking about community endeavours with long historic roots, endeavours that call on us to uncover our better selves.

I'll go further and suggest that houses of worship and houses of baseball serve similar if not identical functions, namely the promise of a safe place of assembly from which to organize our efforts to reach something higher. They offer sensations like few other things in this life do, a sense of the uncanny, heaping doses of wonder, and the tingle on the skin that occurs when we find ourselves in the presence of something that makes possible the miraculous.

There is a feeling I get just before a summer rain interrupts a warm day, a sense- and emotion-memory so strong it's like teleportation: I am just days shy of my 13th birthday and, in the manner of all people that age, on the cusp of so much I cannot anticipate and yet for which I remain both eager and reticent. I am with my parents outside Doubleday Field, the tiny brick ballpark just a block from the Hall of Fame in Cooperstown, where my parents have taken me for my birthday. Everything hums. The warm August day has turned dark and the sky threatens. The pavement smells warm, and seems to know it will soon be wet and black with rain. Soon we'll venture up the little grandstand and watch a half-inning of a little league game being played there. In 18 years I'll stand on this very spot holding my first child and point out Ferguson Jenkins as he signs autographs. That first afternoon, the one when I'm almost 13, the rain is coming but it has not arrived yet, and my mother and father have given this to me. This place, this experience. Baseball is being played, and I have just seen the Hall of Fame for the first time, and Doubleday Field is built of brick and it offers welcome, its roofed grandstand saying, *Even if the sky breaks, I will keep you dry*. In the confluence of all these things I locate a feeling like safety such as I have not felt since infancy.

Twenty-six years later I'm still there in many ways. Worshipful, reverent, and certain that my lifetime of watching and studying this game has not revealed to me all its secrets; that several more lifetimes would leave still more mysteries. And I'm grateful that, though I have permitted so much wonder to be drummed from me, allowed my capacity for sincere surprise to ebb away, I have maintained those feelings where baseball is concerned. It has not lost any of its ability to awe me; when I watch I'm still that kid.

The ballpark is where my otherwise firm secular humanism begins to grow soft, to give out at its edges, to take on a porousness into which seeps something very like belief. It's the place where my weariness and cynicism abate, replaced by an openness and desire for grace. I've followed that feeling to all manner of places. Like a pole star it has determined my direction. I've forgone Paris in favour of Chicago, Seattle, and Allentown, Pennsylvania. I've passed over London for Milwaukee, Phoenix, and Burlington, Vermont. I've tithed it my meagre funds. I've felt wonder at seeing a champion crowned—ascending to the game's heaven, as it were—and then known the despair of the season ending, followed by the reliable joy of the day pitchers and catchers first report to Spring Training, and finally registered the elation of Opening Day, with its unsubtle suggestion of rebirth.

It shows us what a human being might be capable of, with extreme dedication—for if we can't beatify Jackie Robinson or Roberto Clemente then who among us is worthy? We also learn daily just how complicated our lesser saints are, how conflicted and human. Such doubt, of course, confirms faith. Josh Hamilton erred and then righted himself, achieving years of sobriety before a second slip, which he himself reported. Angels owner Arte Moreno cast him out but the Rangers accepted him back into the fold. After that dark hour, Arlington's Globe Life Park probably felt like a sanctuary for Hamilton. He hit a double on the first pitch he saw and two homers the next night. If that's not grace.

Across 9 innings, through 162 games, season after season and decade after decade, baseball asks for devotion, attention, dedication, and it rewards with clemency. It hints that faith and patience and penance will eventually yield pennants, though some paths to the promised land are more arduous than others. In this devising, Chicago Cubs fans represent the most hardcore of ascetics. Here is where that old synagogue in South Bend doubly proves its provenance, for those Midwest League Cubs are but several rungs down the same ladder as the long-suffering North Siders, and the world the Cubbies inhabit is most certainly an Old Testament one.

What other aspect of contemporary life is so imbued with as much quasi-religious ritual as baseball? What other game or pursuit or distraction offers so many symbols? It even has consecrated ground—how else to explain why on a tour of Fenway the groundskeeper insisted we not step on the grass? That, we understood, was turf made hallow by the feet of Jimmie Foxx, Ted Williams, Jim Rice, Carl Yastrzemski.

In terms of both its textual record and the imagery it produces, provokes, and inspires, the richness and abundance of baseball is hard to match outside the ecclesiastical realm. In *Bull Durham*, Susan Sarandon's Annie speaks of "the Church of baseball," and she's right in locating the part of the soul touched by the game as the same one that makes prayer so satisfying. Baseball readily and reliably offers a feeling of reverence so clear and deep it can't be discounted.

The brain seeks defense mechanisms to inveigh against all manner of threat, from boredom to suspicions of futility, so it might be that in the face of baseball's sheer volume—its frequent lulls, the endurance that's required to withstand an entire campaign—we have become adept at imbuing it with unearned meaning and significance. It *might* be that the only answer to the question, *What is it about this game?*

is that it grinds us down long enough to render impotent our otherwise sharp and clinical sensibilities. But I don't think so, and I suspect that if you do, you might as well quit reading now, because most of these essays spring from the tacit awareness that baseball vibrates with something a little strange, that it trembles with a bit of stuff we might as well call magic for our inability to fully articulate it. This conviction is necessary to me, as it keeps me going during a blowout in early June between two teams whose lacklustre fates have been determined since mid-April; the deep belief that even if *this* game means nothing, this *game* still means something.

It shouldn't be necessary to state a fact so obvious, but just to be safe let me underline it: I watch baseball a certain way, but that doesn't for a second have any bearing on how you take it in. No interloper is required to intervene between you and the object of your devotion, no member of an ordained class need shape your relationship to the game. You're free to love it in your own way, and you don't need homogeneous talking heads or beat reporters to confer their blessings upon you. You don't need bloggers, stat-heads, season-ticket holders or self-appointed experts, and you sure as hell don't need me. It's yours as surely as it is mine, and it asks chiefly for your attention in whatever form that takes.

But for me, baseball is epiphanic, a contemplative tedium interrupted by bursts of significant action. It's the impossible made infrequently possible. Long intervals spent wandering the desert and sudden inexplicable miracles. I'm willing to concede there's some Plato too in the symmetry of the dimensions, the cleanness of the rules being as close to perfection as we're permitted to get, echoes of an ideal that exists off-camera and is ultimately untouchable.

The exercise, or indulgence, of all this requires a steadfast refusal to permit corruption in Major League Baseball's organizational structure to mar said belief. It requires making allowances for the earthbound politics and prejudices of the people who run the game while maintaining the divinity and perfection of the game itself. Collusion, tax dodging, inequality in hiring practices, the exclusion of women, the "gentleman's agreement" that prevented non-white players from participating, rule changes including but not limited to the designated hitter, the movement of franchises, the invention of Astroturf... all are regrettable but attributable to human fallibility, while the game itself continues unhampered.

Whatever our clumsy efforts, however we might muck it up, I tune in to a game to satisfy the desire to witness something uncanny, a desire so fervent it becomes need. And I suppose that's as likely an inspiration for religion as any other you might conjure.

And like religion, the feeling is strongest within its designated houses of assembly. My "home" ballpark—90 minutes away from my house, give or take—is the Rogers Centre in Toronto, which is only proof that some houses are more beautiful than others. They can't all be the Sistine Chapel. Whatever their form—tiny or massive, domed or open, concrete or wood or brick, or bleachers made from aluminum—ballparks are host to something so spiritually, aesthetically, emotionally, and intellectually stimulating as to elevate them, whatever their architectural shortcomings. They, by dint of the proceedings they host, are redolent of beauty.

"Baseball is a hard game: love it hard and it will love you back hard," said Pete Rose. Its arduous rhythms lend structure and rigidity to life, or at least half of it, roughly April through October. It repays sustained attention, accommodates our mistakes, provides shelter despite our slips. It will bend to us if we bend to it. In short, it offers the same rewards as most faiths. Baseball's allure lies in all the tricks it has already shown us and all the tricks it might yet deliver.

Visitors to the South Bend Cubs' team store are greeted with a verse from Exodus written on the wall. "Make for me a sanctuary," it reads, "and I will dwell in their midst." Apply that to baseball any way you wish. That sanctuaries exist so we might dwell in them, or that baseball might dwell in them with us as its witnesses, or that sanctuaries represent portals offering us access to something higher and more perfect. For me, what's salient is that the word "sanctuary" is the right one, that the sense of safety and welcome and shelter I experience in passing through the turnstile is not one I experience alone. It tells me there is something substantial at play in those places, and that the language of mysticism and belief I affix to baseball is not entirely misplaced. It says that feeling is real, and that it's the reason so many of us are inspired to offer such devotion. It's why the Fenway Park organist, after Carlton Fisk won Game 6 of the '75 Series by waving his home run fair, began playing Handel's "Hallelujah" chorus. It's why when we talk about baseball, unavoidably, we talk about going home.

THE UTILITY OF BOREDOM

Things sounded tedious in Viera. The crowd was thin, disinterested. The PA echoed. A foul ball was struck, arced up toward the broadcast booth, then fell into the stands. "The folks down there have been asleep the better part of an hour," said the colour commentator, "that'll wake them up."

This was on the radio, or rather the Internet, or rather the radio via the Internet. I was busy doing nothing. It was late in the spring, when the calendar says it's technically no longer winter but up here there's snow hanging on in the shadows and you don't want to be out past dark without gloves and a coat. But it was a sunny day, I remember. Life, I was thinking, is long and blissfully empty. I folded laundry, scrubbed pots.

The Nationals were playing the Astros in Viera, Florida and I could not have cared less about the outcome. That wasn't the point. Neither was catching up on the prospects both teams would be running out onto the field in 2012. The Nats were ascending then while the Astros were not. It was late Spring Training and the decisions, mostly, had been made. The regulars' goal was to strike a balance between getting in their pre-season work and avoiding injury. There was still a supply of fringe guys, men in uniform whose fates had already been decided but who remained on hand to fill in once the everyday players had put in a few innings. When all this was over and the teams headed north the fill-in players would be right back in the bus leagues. Everybody knew this. Nobody had much left to prove. This was ritual largely devoid of meaning. It was players playing because a schedule told them they were meant to play. By the time the announcers began admitting they had no idea who was on the field because the fill-ins' names weren't in the media guide, it occurred to me that this was baseball as devised by Tom Stoppard. It was boring and beautiful, and radio was the perfect medium to convey it, allowing me to futz absentmindedly around the house with the sound of the play-by-play drifting through rooms and down hallways.

Modern televised baseball is a marvel, crystal clear and stacked with reams of information, and I don't take it for granted. But it can also be overwhelming. Radio broadcasts, on the other hand, are unfailingly comforting.

There used to be an element of providence involved in picking up a game on the radio; a small joy that registered when a signal drifted across the Great Lakes intact or bounced at just the right angle off the troposphere and came in—hallelujah!—clear as day. There was something viscerally satisfying about knowing where in your house to prop a radio or where to pilot your sedan, to which hills, in order to ensure the best reception. Sometimes, on summer nights, I'd drive my old Saturn down the highways of Eastern Ontario and when I let the dial scan it would pick up not just Blue Jays games but broadcasts from New York, Pittsburgh, Philadelphia, Cleveland. We've traded all that for the ability, provided we've ponied up the subscription fee, to reliably tune in KMOX from St. Louis, KLAC from Los Angeles, KCSP from Kansas City, or KIRO from Seattle. That's progress: we lose chance but gain convenience.

At 10 or 12 years of age I'd go to sleep listening to the Blue Jays on AM radio. I was struck then and remain so by the idea that the radio waves that make up those broadcasts are working their way through the cosmos steadily and so will always exist somewhere, capturable, even if not from here. Every game! An O-fer by Rance Mulliniks and that time the Jays hit ten homers against the Orioles. They're all out there, floating, advancing, eternal invisible waves of sound spreading baseball out into the farthest, darkest, quietest corners of the universe.

And yet, despite that literally universal reach, radio possesses an intimacy that makes it ideally suited to depict baseball's essential boredom.

I don't see a problem hanging the word "boredom" around baseball's neck. Nor do I see it as an epithet. Boredom is fertile. Boredom is potential. Boredom is the basic element of all of baseball's drama.

Each game lasts at least nine innings. Twenty-seven outs a side. Hundreds of pitches and, consequently, hundreds of interstitial moments of adjustment, collection, sign-shaking. Hundreds of instances of a player standing stock still on the mound holding a ball, facing a second player holding a bat and standing equally still, or perhaps waving the end of the bat around in little circles over his head.

Each season is 162 such games, at minimum.

Now add Spring Training.

That's a *lot* of time. But baseball can make you feel like you've got time to burn. These days that's a precious feeling. Late capitalism has proved to be okay, I guess, but mostly a big headache, with more batteries to keep charged and more bullshit vying for our eyes and ears than at any other point in human history. It's the Golden Age of

Distraction and it's rewiring us with hair-trigger attention spans. I grow easily bored and quickly anxious that I'm missing something entertaining. Technology feeds this. *Like cute animals?* the Internet asks. *Okay, here's 13,000 more adorable videos.*

Baseball's a chore by comparison. It promises no satisfying outcome, only nine grinding innings, the same troughs of inaction studded with brief explosions of motion. Boredom is integral, in-built. You can't sustain unfettered excitement for 162 games. It would be ludicrous to try. The baseball season is more gruelling than that of any other sport. It's more of a marathon than a marathon. Both basketball's back-and-forth and hockey's flair and brutality are confined to 82 games. Those sports feature a fairly exaggerated ratio of crescendo to diminuendo; they exist at a ratcheted level of excitement that borders on the surreal. Baseball's peaks, meanwhile, are so grand because its valleys are so broad and deep. Imagine lazily going about your business on a vacant spring afternoon while tuned in to a hockey game. The vibe and the setting don't sync.

Boredom, in the baseball sense, is a synonym for lackadaisical; it's the only proper response to all that green grass and blue sky. Slouchy in the Viera stands, the beery patrons were in no hurry to shake the peanut shells from their hair and return to real life. They wanted to sprawl over those sticky plastic seats for which they'd paid. And the players—the unknown pitcher on the mound palming the ball mindlessly, the batter stepping in, stepping out, stepping back in, adjusting his cup, a batting glove, his helmet—were happy to oblige.

This is where good radio announcers truly shine: filling the space. I once heard Vin Scully—who is the all-time best and, though he also works the TV side of things now, earned his stripes doing radio in Brooklyn—describing a cloud over Dodger Stadium and it was the most riveting and moving 30 seconds of the entire broadcast. It's for this reason too that baseball became a game of such minute statistical detail: that folks at microphones should have something to say when there was nothing to discuss and nothing happening on the field.

The announcers in Viera were overmatched, frankly, so the middle and late innings of the game were a trial by inaction. Sometimes baseball tests you as a fan with boredom that's less mellow and more murderous. But the seeds of excitement are tucked into such loam, are watered and nurtured there. That's the investment that sustains fans, the knowledge that afternoons such as that one—four baskets of laundry to fold, a third baseman no one can identify—make possible days like September 28, 2011, perhaps the most exciting day of regular-season baseball the world has ever seen. The Rays surmounted a seven-run deficit to beat the Yankees in extras, propelled by a bottom of the ninth homer from pinch-hitter Dan Johnson and two slow trots for Evan Longoria, while at the very same time in Baltimore the Red Sox coughed up game 162 to the then-lowly Orioles, completing the greatest September choke job in history. In the National League, the Phillies were going into extras too where they would eventually beat the Braves, while the Cardinals were thumping on Houston, thereby delivering St. Louis a Wild Card spot and sending Atlanta home to a long off-season. All in one evening.

It's the awareness of such possibilities that tempers the dullness. You have to think of the long game. Baseball's an exercise in concentration, a chance to train the brain to ignore the echoes of other forms of entertainment offering easier enticements. You sit through nine innings because that's how long a game is and you want to watch a game. You sit through blowouts. You endure a game devoid of offense and call it a pitchers' duel. When attending you show up early and stay until the final out is recorded, transit schedules and traffic be damned. This is your quiet commitment. This is your loyalty and your investment, your faith that every recess and concavity will eventually be mirrored by something amazing. Slow and steady, you say.

It's a long season but the winter is longer. Life, despite our efforts to decorate its every surface, to bedeck it in glitz and colour, is often boring. Though we distract ourselves in order to try to forget as much, death most certainly looms. But the meantime is better with baseball than it would be without it.

When my children are starved for stimulation they tell me, "There's nothing to do."

"So do nothing," I tell them.

What a luxury and what a happy thing, to be alive. That's what I'm really feeling when I listen to a game. How lucky I am to be bored. That's how it felt listening to the game in Viera, folding clothes, hearing the announcers shake off winter's rust, the players getting loose for the long, long season ahead. I thought: Hear the game! Summer is possible! Baseball!

THE 163 GAMES
OF JOSÉ OQUENDO

José Oquendo played second base on a good Cardinals team in 1989. The switch-hitting Puerto Rican had come up as a shortstop, drafted by the Mets to play there, but when traded to the Cardinals in '85 he found himself blocked by Ozzie Smith. So he did whatever was asked of him, played anywhere there was a spot, and became known for his versatility. In '87 he appeared at every position but catcher (he got a chance to catch a game in '88). A spot finally opened at second in '89 and he grabbed it. It was his best season. He set career marks in nearly every offensive category and proved a solid defender, committing only five errors across the entire season. That's the other remarkable thing about José Oquendo's 1989: he shared the National League lead in the category of games played.

There is no reason to give him any thought now except that in the week before Opening Day I'm prone to some strange behavior, including salvaging a hellish family trip to Target by grabbing a mystery pack of baseball cards—100 cards for $5—from a rack near the cash and sifting through them while my wife drives us all home. It was an odd collection of cards spanning the years 1980 to 2010, including All-Stars and a good number of players I'd more or less forgotten (Mackey Sasser!). There were cards put out by Topps, Fleer, Bowman, and Upper Deck, as well as singles from strange sets I'd never before seen. But, however improbably, among all the Hall of Famers (8 of the 100 cards, including Bruce Sutter and Eddie Murray), and those soon to be Cooperstown-bound and for whom cases can be made (Roger Clemens, Jack Morris, Chipper Jones), it was José Oquendo's card that got my attention.

I was, like a lot of kids my age, pretty serious about baseball cards for a time, even allowing myself to be seduced by the notion that somewhere in those wax packs or the display cases of my local card shop there was the million-dollar card that would deliver me an easy life. During the hobby's bubble in the early '90s—when shops opened everywhere, conventions came annually to large local venues, and every drugstore stocked fresh copies of the *Beckett Baseball Card Monthly* pricing guide—it was hard to find a boy who wasn't a collector and who didn't harbour dreams of wealth similar to my own. None of us had ever actually met anyone who'd gotten rich off the hobby but some apocryphal knowledge had worked its way down to us, perhaps from the men working the tables at those conventions, or the woman and her son who ran the local sports memorabilia store, and so we were convinced it was possible.

   I never sold a card. I still have them all. The riches eluded me as they did most everyone. Too many people had the same idea and too many cards were made. Adults elbowed their way into a kids' hobby and nothing was quite the same afterward. The bubble burst. All it left me was a few years' worth of complete sets, a copy of the infamous Billy Ripken "FUCK FACE" card which I keep in a strongbox with passports and other important documents, and a habit of examining cards like a forensic scientist when they fall into my possession. This is the natural result, I'm convinced, of having used them as a source of information in the pre-Internet era. They were a tool in the kit of the informed fan, along with the annual *Who's Who in Baseball* guide, the season preview magazines, and careful attention paid to your team's radio and TV broadcasts. Cards were how we learned about players. We studied them and we memorized them. Even now, when I stumble across the name of a marginal or forgotten player from the era, it's not unusual for me to recall with startling clarity the pose they struck on their '88 Topps card or their '90 Upper Deck.

I haven't been an active collector for over 20 years but every now and then, usually in the early spring when my need for baseball is most acute, I'll buy a pack. They're no longer displayed in a box on the counter at convenience stores and there is no more chalky gum in the wax paper package. But they're around and I'll pick up a pack just to sift through its offerings, smiling at All-Stars and up-and-comers, getting a bit wistful when an old favourite shows up, a guy hanging on at the end of his career. This is all that's left now, a residual tick, a ritual frivolity meant to ease the transition from deep winter to benevolent spring. I'll pore over them, sort them, and then pass them on to my kids, who'll destroy them in a matter of minutes.

But while studying the motley deck I purchased from Target in a raucous minivan headed home from a shopping trip, I saw something that struck me as odd on the back of José Oquendo's '92 Topps. I must have initially noticed the card for its tiny, stretched-out panoramic photo of the old Busch Stadium, but above the photo, among the stats in that bold and italicized font Topps used to designate a league leader in a given statistical category, the asymmetrical number *163* appeared under the G column.

How, I wondered, had José Oquendo managed to play one more game than his St. Louis Cardinals team did?

It's an anomalous feat, as it turns out, but it's not unheard of. Thirty players have recorded seasons of more than 162 games, led by Maury Wills for the '61 Dodgers. Wills logged 165 games that year, as the Dodgers played a three-game playoff against the Giants (who else?) and he saw action in every game. The more common ways of accomplishing the trick are by getting yourself traded to a team that's played fewer games to that point, and by having a game or two called due to weather. The latter was the case with Oquendo. One of the quirks of baseball scoring holds that players get credit for things done (and not done) even if a game must be replayed. It's another of those strange little things that makes baseball, and all its associated arcana, impossible not to love. Among those who've played more than 162 games you'll find players you'd expect, including a few who did it twice: Billy Williams, Brooks Robinson, and Pete Rose, which is fitting, as all three were guys who'd have played doubleheaders eight days a week if they'd found a way to do it. There are also unexpected members of the 163-Game Club, like Oquendo, and fellow Cardinal Todd Zeile who did it in 1996.

Adding further intrigue is the fact that Oquendo shared the NL lead for games played in '89. A bit of digging yields Bobby Bonilla's name as the co-leader. Bonilla did it the same way—stats for an incomplete contest, thus logging 163 games for the Pirates that year. The Pittsburgh third baseman was an All-Star and earned some MVP votes. Oquendo enjoyed no such honours but he was a vital cog on a Cardinals team that was in a dogfight with the Mets and Cubs for much of that summer. In the end they fell short, winding up in third while Chicago's 93 wins took the East. The Cardinals, with much of their '87 pennant-winning roster still intact, flirted with the top in '89 by amassing a couple of five-game win streaks but never really put it all together. But you can't blame that on José Oquendo.

I'm in the habit of looking to baseball for meaning, a Tao, a design for living. It's likely a faulty approach to life but I'd venture it's not the worst. Accordingly, I have felt myself judged by Jim Eisenreich, buoyed by Marco Scutaro's persistence, and heartened by Ichiro's consistency. Accidentally, unexpectedly, I came across José Oquendo's feat and it too now occupies a spot on this list of inspirations. He showed up every day. It's not the only thing he did, certainly, and it was as much a product of luck, good health, and manager Whitey Herzog's decisions as it was Oquendo's effort. But it's admirable just the same, a testament to determination, patience, and drive. There was a time when José Oquendo was a fringe player, a man without a position. That would defeat a lot of us. But Oquendo adapted and in time he earned his spot. Once he had it, he did all in his power to keep it. Hell, the man played 163 games. You can't ask more than that.

THE BALLPARKS OF AMERICA

The ballparks of America are open for business. In Chicago, in Des Moines, in Batavia, New York. They have unlocked their turnstiles and they await the gathering crowds. Their concourses are swept, their concession stands stocked, their playing surfaces watered, cut, swept, raked, painted.

In the ballparks of America—brick beauties in big cities, small diamonds with aluminum bleachers among Midwest cornfields, forgotten wooden grandstands with Rocky Mountain backdrops—you are treated to the aromatic bouquet of roasted peanuts, hot dogs and beer, grass, sunblock, the peppery smell of smokers in their designated areas on the concourse. In the ballparks of America you can gaze upon the impossible green of coddled grass, the endless blue of an afternoon sky, or the blinding white glare of lights on their stanchions carving artificial daylight out of velvety summer darkness. In the ballparks of America you can sit next to Americans and it's the closest you will come to being let into their homes. It's a cultural point of entry, into Budweiser, heckling, and how romance operates in the United States. The slouch-pantsed, flat-brimmed, tattooed young men who aren't on the field drape an arm over the soft, round shoulders of girls who may one day soon give them children, and your heart is at once hopeful and sad on their behalf.

When sweet high summer is almost here the ballparks of America begin their siren calls, tempting you south to such exotic locales as Burlington, Vermont, and Cincinnati, Ohio, and Cedar Rapids, Iowa. In heeding their beckoning you may find yourself someplace new or you may return to places you already know and remember with both fondness and despair.

In Great Falls, Montana it's 110 degrees and the mascot, in a plush jackrabbit costume, in the fullness of the Great Plains' heat, refuses to move. The jackrabbit plunks itself down at the end of your row and puts its feet up. Daylight leaves but the heat does not. Great Falls beats the Billings Mustangs and you clap and wipe your brow and head out into the suffocating night. At the Motel 6 you crank the air and fall asleep watching *Baseball Tonight*.

In Sanford, Maine a woman tells you what the mill closures have done to the town and how there are no tourist dollars because Sanford is so far inland. Orchard Beach catches all the tourists. But Sanford has its little ballpark proudly bearing a "Babe Ruth was here" plaque, and it has a summer collegiate team, the Mainers, in bright gold and kelly green uniforms. You sit in the covered grandstand and eat caramel corn and ice cream sandwiches and cheer on a kid who'll be in The Show in a few years' time.

In Spokane, Washington your ticket is drawn and you win a free one-year membership to a local gym, the only prize you have won in your life. Though Spokane is lovely, you live several time zones away and so must decline.

At Spring Training facilities in Arizona the sun is so intense there are sunscreen dispensers in the washrooms. In the swampy Florida heat you cool yourself beneath a spray of misted water while you watch non-roster invitees wearing numbers like 98 attempt to unseat a veteran and steal a place on the bench of an actual major league team.

In Auburn, New York the rain comes early and ends the game but they still launch the Fourth of July fireworks afterward into the upstate sky while the teenage members of the grounds crew recline on the pitcher's mound and take it all in.

In Seattle, from your seat high up in the Safeco Field stands, you can see Mt. Rainier as well as Félix Hernández. Both are astonishing.

On Chicago's north side, though their boys are down 14 runs, Cubs fans cheer a single home team run as though it were a game winner, which goes a long way toward explaining what a century of futility can do to a group of people. The hot dogs are good, anyway, heaped with onions. In the ballparks of America there's always something to eat even if the game is lousy.

In Syracuse the trains rumble by the fence in left, shaking the remaining mortar from the brickwork of abandoned factories.

In Boston they'll throw their Sam Adams at you for wearing Yankees gear, which seems like a terrible way to waste a beer.

At Yankee Stadium you want to pay your respects to Miller Huggins but they closed the gates to Monument Park 90 minutes before game time, so the Rays' 7–1 victory is all the more sweet. Celebrities sit in the first row right behind the dugout while you and your father make do with nosebleeds over left field.

In Philadelphia they boo when a Mets batter fouls a ball off his foot and needs a moment to allow the pain to subside, and then they boo louder when he's okay.

In Baltimore you discover that Camden Yards is one of the more beautiful spots on Earth, though if you happen by when Boston is visiting the place is overrun with Sox fans, squawking like groundbirds flushed from the undergrowth. Before the first pitch the crab shacks are full of New Englanders ordering another round in their lovely, ridiculous accents.

In Los Angeles they beat a man into a coma for wearing a Giants jersey.

In Allentown, Pennsylvania you see none of the restlessness Billy Joel described; everyone seems perfectly happy to stay, to eat corn dogs and watch the IronPigs turn unpolished young men into potential Phillies.

In the ballparks of America you cannot imagine the courage required to be a woman in the presence of so many men with beer in their hands and in their heads.

In the ballparks of America you have seen and can see again the best of America, and the indifferent, and the worst. In the ballparks of America you may feel as though you are close to understanding America, or maybe just Americans, as you sit shoulder to shoulder with them and sip beer, keep score, and question a called strike. You can focus on the things you agree on: the game on the field, those who have played it before, and those who are playing it now. The beer is too expensive, you might say, but still we're lucky to be here, and they'll nod in accord. Whatever happens after the final out, wherever the congregants may scatter, it's worth remembering that.

GET ME OVER

At first you could only do it underhanded, with a straight wrist and "for the bat," meaning throw it where they can hit it. In 1883, after the sidearm curveball had been developed and permitted, the rule makers dropped the pretence. They allowed overhand throwing and accepted that the pitcher's job was to get hitters out. In 1893 they moved the pitcher from 50 feet away to 60 feet 6 inches and the modern discipline was more or less established. The game we know took shape. If it's hard to imagine what a hitter might do with a 102 mph Aroldis Chapman heater from a distance of only 50 feet, it's because we've had more than 130 years to get used to things the way they are at present.

Pitching has changed during that period—role specialization, the cut fastball, medical advances, analytic video study, banning the spitball, and so forth—but the broad philosophy and aim remains precisely as it was then: throw strikes, get hitters out, keep the other guys from scoring. Pitchers have enjoyed eras of dominance (the dead-ball era, the 1960s) then been put in check by tweaks (changes to the makeup of the ball, smaller parks, and Babe Ruth in the case of the former; lowering the mound from 15 inches to 10 inches for the latter). Pitching may win games but offense is what sells tickets; pitchers are, in some sense, in inherent opposition to baseball's very makeup. This is not a new thing, of course, but in a stretch during which pitchers have emphatically dominated hitters it feels especially urgent. What has been clear throughout the game's whole turbulent history is that pitchers comprise a very different sort of human being. They're not quite like the other people who play baseball for a living and they're not quite like the rest of us either.

Pitchers are touched in some way. Most of us can't imagine accepting the sort of pressure a pitcher endures, or being willing to throw a baseball in the direction of Giancarlo Stanton, in full awareness of what Giancarlo Stanton routinely does to baseballs. Who would choose this?

It makes sense, given those odds and the murderous intent of the bat-wielding men they face, that pitchers would create their own mythology. Inside the fraternity, they are curators and practitioners and lay priests of an ancient art, though the game they play isn't yet two centuries old.

Perhaps they recognize their role as alchemists, participants in an inexact discipline, one requiring as much guesswork as knowledge, and enough courage and confidence to patch the gap between the two. To be a pitcher is to place one's belief in something bizarre; it therefore fits that the believers themselves are somewhat bizarre. They could not be what they are, or do what they do, if they were not.

Mordecai Brown had three (and one gnarled half) fingers on his hurling hand but decided pitching was a viable career option anyway. Cy Young had a sixth-grade education but was so gifted at his chosen craft that he coached pitchers at Harvard. Walter Johnson is the second-winningest pitcher in history but openly tossed meatballs to his buddy Sam Crawford of the Tigers; they're both in the Hall of Fame. After the final out of the 1955 World Series, Sandy Koufax drove himself to Columbia University to attend class. I'm not even touching on the various pre-Eisenhower Dizzys and Dazzys here, nor pausing to examine more recent fringe elements such as tooth-brushing Turk Wendell. These are the icons of the craft we're talking about; the establishment was this strange, this different.

Which fits because a pitcher's situation is unique in sport. He leads the defensive team, and yet he holds the ball and is in most ways on the attack. He stands alone whereas the batter is backed up—there's another hitter standing just behind him, waiting his turn. The pitcher perches on a little round hump of earth and all eyes are on him. Nothing happens until he decides it should. He controls everything. This is not defense as we generally understand it. "Good pitching in a close game," Roger Angell once wrote, "is the cement that makes baseball the marvelous, complicated structure that it is."

And yet the pitcher controls so little. Rather, he deals in precarity. He takes his sign, or shakes it off and waits for the one he wants, and then he winds and cocks and swings his arm wild, the muscles and tendons stretched to the very limit of their capacity, and he releases the ball. It rolls off his fingertips and he follows through, and then he too is but a spectator watching the ball churn through space toward the plate. It finds its mark or it doesn't; it's hit with a bat or it isn't; the hit ball lands fair or it lands foul; the fair ball is caught or it isn't. He has done his job or he hasn't.

It's worth remembering that even the very best get hit around on occasion. The ball is struck and the fielders wheel like constellations as the hitter becomes a baserunner. Then the pitcher must return to the mound and summon anew the resolve to do his job, only now with a man dancing off first or the tying run standing on third and nobody out, and the odds now, suddenly, very different.

Little wonder then that these men are frequently unique themselves. They are supermen, often highly valued (and compensated), but living always with the likelihood of terrific failure. They know it sits just around the next bend because they've all seen it just like we have: their successes are beautiful to behold, but when those same pitchers begin to falter they can do so with sudden and awful totality. They seem to be doing the same things they've always done but now with heartbreaking results. The history of baseball is speckled with pitchers who ascended to great heights only to be humbled in their next breath.

Mark "The Bird" Fidrych, the jubilant Tiger whose 2.34 ERA and 19 wins earned him the 1976 Rookie of the Year nod, saw his career go downhill fast after that astonishing campaign. He was out of the majors within five years. Rick Ankiel threw a good fastball and a devastating curve for the Cardinals, starting in 1999 and continuing until the third inning of Game 1 of the 2000 National League Division Series against Atlanta when he suddenly lost the ability to throw strikes, producing one of the most awkwardly unwatchable innings of baseball ever televised. He later reinvented himself as a power-hitting outfielder, eking out another decade in the majors. Barry Zito stands as a recent example of the position's fickleness: an initially dominant pitcher who, at a certain point and for unclear reasons, appeared to simply misplace his mastery of the craft.

These, and hundreds more, some with more striking suddenness than others. The precariousness of their chosen discipline shines a light on our own lives: no matter how good things look, we're all just hanging on by a thread. No matter how in command, no matter how good the stuff, the truth is that we are on defense the entire time and we will eventually be reminded as much.

"Chicks dig the long ball," the commercial said, and though its expression is sexist and frivolous the sentiment is largely valid: most of us, regardless of our gender, choose a favourite player based on what he can do with a bat. Watching a ball travel 420 feet or knowing your guy is likely to knock in the runner on second base: these are satisfying things and their impact on the game's outcome is obvious. Runs are scored and if your team collects more runs than the other team they win. This is how it works, and it makes sense, and we all understand it.

But among us there are those whose hearts race at something so mundane as a fat, get-me-over curveball thrown for a strike in a 3–0 count, or who savour bearing witness to the sweathouse pressure of a closer dealing with a speedy runner on first with two out in the ninth inning of a one-run game. Those drawn to pitchers are so attracted precisely because of the uncertainty outlined above, not in spite of it. Even when a pitcher appears to have the world in his back pocket—Orel Hershiser's 59 straight scoreless innings, Éric Gagné's 84 consecutive saves, Justin Verlander's 24-win Cy Young- and MVP- winning 2011—the game's improbable architecture requires that the threat of failure is never far off. It is, on the contrary, ever present. It's the darkness that makes such bright light so beautiful. Failure is the air that baseball breathes and each matchup, each hitter faced, every pitch, is a chance to fail, and as successes are strung together they become more thrilling because they become increasingly unlikely. The odds mount against that pitcher's continued good luck.

What pitchers do appears to be so simple: chuck a ball over the plate. Do it well and they're successful; do it well long enough and they're fabulously rich to boot. View it that way and there are very few external factors to bear on success or failure. A pitcher must do only one thing and if he does not do it well the consequences are clear. Those among us who strive to live in ways that are similarly simple and authentic are drawn to the practical obviousness. The pitcher's craft may rely upon craftiness but there is no masking the result. He succeeds until he fails, and then he has to go out there and do it again. It's an emotionally punishing undertaking, masochistic even, and it breeds opportunities for a raking of one's pride plainly familiar to most any human resident of planet Earth.

Modern pitching is analytic and sterilized, subject to biometric analysis and pitch counts, and increasingly backed up by defensive shifts gleaned from spray charts. But the guts of the thing remain unchanged: on each pitch one player is responsible for his team's fate. The pitcher holds the ball and then he releases it into a destiny he only faintly controls; if he's good, the score remains the same. If his mechanics are off, if his release point is inconsistent, or if he's lost contact with the mysterious forces that determine how a ball dances through air, things change drastically.

Pitchers all contain the seeds of their own undoing and they all hold within themselves a shot at redemption. Another hitter. Another inning. They stare down failure to find deliverance. Those of us whose favourite ballplayers do their work on a mound move through the world knowing that, at some point, we're all pitchers. They are the beautiful, tragic stand-ins for our lives and their work is not so different from our own.

So we cheer for them and, in so doing, encourage ourselves. This is sport's most basic mission: to show us what we can do and outline the limits of our abilities in order to motivate us to stretch them. So we hump fastballs into the catcher's mitt, hacking at success while suspecting defeat. We might want to hold onto the ball, to halt the world, but eventually we must let it go. That's the exhilarating truth, the terrifying truth. We must let it leave our fingertips and spin out into space and then, in that interminable moment, we can only await the results.

JIM EISENREICH'S EYES

In the summer of 1988 I stole a pack of baseball cards. I was
11 years old and my parents and I were staying with cousins
in a small borrowed cottage nestled among the dunes
and pine just north of Wasaga Beach, Ontario. I was not
generally prone to such behaviour, but it happened. I was in
the company of my younger cousin, Krista, and her friend,
whose name I don't remember, but let's call her Jennifer. It
was morning and we had made the short walk down the
beach and up a sandy, shaded path to the convenience store
where we routinely bought our Cokes and Freezies and
Twizzlers, as well as the marshmallows we'd roast over fires
on the beach. It was a mom-and-pop place, a small house
converted by the use of plywood and linoleum into a place
for cottagers to buy their milk.

While Krista and Jennifer chose their candy and browsed
magazines, oohing over photos of Chad Allen or River
Phoenix in a copy of *Tiger Beat*, I located my quarry: the
open box of O-Pee-Chee baseball cards tucked on a shelf
near the back of the store instead of its more traditional spot
near the cash. It had not been my intent upon entering the
store to slip into a life of crime. But I felt the pull of those
cards, entrenched as I then was in a sort of baseball mania,
and I saw an opportunity—an opening, like the parting of
clouds. I didn't have enough money, but suddenly I had
the perfect moment, a fold in the fabric of time, dark and

hidden, while Krista and Jennifer paid for their things. I slid the wax paper package into the pocket of my shorts. As we strode home through the sand I pulled the pack from my pocket and began to unwrap it. Krista, chewing a Twizzler, said, "Where'd you get that?"

"At the store," I said.

She looked at me sternly and sized up the situation. "That wasn't good," she said.

"Don't tell," I said pleadingly.

"I won't," she said, and I knew she wouldn't. In a small family we were the only children of similar age, a bond we took seriously. We kept our secrets.

Truthfully, I felt pretty good in that moment, under the bright sun, the summer-warmed waters of Georgian Bay lapping at my feet and my boosted prize waiting to reveal to me its contents. I popped the chalky stick of gum in my mouth and turned over the stack of cards. And there, staring up at me with cold, judging eyes, was Jim Eisenreich.

James Michael Eisenreich is a symbol of perseverance, a man who, by virtue of his experiences, possesses a great moral heft. And Eisenreich, as evidenced by the photo adorning his 1988 O-Pee-Chee card, has eyes capable of conveying all of that.

A first baseman who could play the outfield or slide to DH if required, Jim Eisenreich didn't have much pop in his bat but he could hit for a decent average. He's best known for his time with the Phillies, especially '93 when he hit .318 and helped them take the NL pennant, as well as the career year he had in '96—.361 AVG/413 OBP/.476 SLG—on a last-place Phils team that was well into a post-pennant slide. He signed with Florida that off-season and two years later—

after winning the '97 Series—was part of the blockbuster that brought Mike Piazza and Todd Zeile to Miami.

Those would be the most remarkable things about Eisenreich's career were it not for the voluntary exile from the game he took from 1984 until he returned for the '87 campaign. Drafted by the Twins in 1980, the Minnesota native struggled in parts of three major league seasons to overcome Tourette syndrome before opting to leave baseball. But the game drew him back and the Royals snatched him off waivers after the '86 season.

It was as a Royal that I first knew of him, a steely-eyed presence on baseball cards and a name mentioned now and then on Blue Jays broadcasts. I knew his story, either from those broadcasts or from the baseball magazines I read with fervent devotion. He was the focus of much admiration, lauded for his courage and strength, the determination to do what he wanted no matter the hand dealt him. He was, as a result, perfectly qualified to judge the souls of others, or so it seemed to me as I stared down at that baseball card. Jim Eisenreich, I felt, was staring into my very beating heart, weighing my character and finding me lacking.

Mine was a crime of convenience. Not daring, not conviction, not a desire to impress. It came at the dawn of a time in life when nothing feels determined and everything seems possible. Will I be a criminal? Possibly. Will I be a saint? A doctor, rapper, teacher, meteorologist? I had no answers. I might have been trying out a way of life. I might have been acting on simple impulse. I might simply have wanted that pack of cards very badly.

In the end I found that I didn't have the stomach for it. I didn't go back for more. I wasn't proud. Neither was I courageous; I failed to come clean, didn't return to the store to turn in the goods. I just kept quiet, went home, added the cards, including Eisenreich's, to the growing stash kept beneath my bed. Krista never told anyone, as far as I know, and this is the first time I've ever admitted it.

It was a long time ago and it amounted to nothing, but the memory is clear to me, almost hot to the touch, and connected inextricably with Jim Eisenreich's eyes, their power to bore right through me, then as now. I'm tempted to say the memory would not feel so weighted, even at this remove, had I found Bobby Bonilla smiling back at me from the top of that stack of cards, or Darryl Strawberry, or anybody else. But something about Eisenreich's eyes, and the story of his struggle and ultimate triumph, seemed to indicate that he possessed the gravity and grace that I, the petty thief, did not. What's more, his unblinking stare suggested I might never achieve his strength of character, that my transgressions would come to define me across the long years that lay ahead.

Jim Eisenreich didn't scare me straight. I was not moved by his example to lead a better life. I simply felt wrong, having done what I did, and so did not do it anymore. But he's a part of this memory for me, staring out at me from that 1988 card with his conjuror's eyes. There is something priestly about his pose. He is stoic, sombre, composed.

And now, when I think of Jim Eisenreich, I think of that summer and the things I was learning about myself then. About how I was capable of harbouring unchildlike secrets. About how the landscape of my character seemed to be taking on a new topography. And about how I felt unexpectedly but inevitably propelled forward into things that I knew, even then, resembled the routine moral uncertainties that awaited me—that awaited all of us—in adulthood.

THE BEST THAT I COULD DO

Theodore Roosevelt Lilly III was a good lefty—big, looping curveball and a plodding but accurate fastball—who bounced around a bit: Expos, Yankees, A's, Jays, Cubs, Dodgers. Back when he was still just a minor leaguer from Lomita, California I sold him a John Mellencamp CD. He'd been drafted by the Dodgers and then shipped to the Expos. As he worked his way up the chain toward the bigs he landed in Ottawa, where I encountered him at a CD store in a strip mall on St. Laurent Boulevard. He bought a copy of Mellencamp's greatest hits package, *The Best That I Could Do*, and if you went in search of a descriptor to hang on Lilly's career you could do worse than that.

As a baseball nut I knew who Ted Lilly was but out of context I didn't recognize him—when he approached the cash counter with a disc in his hand he was just a guy with an accent I'd have described as southern. I rang up his sale, took his cash, handed him some change, and asked him if he wanted a bag. He left the store.

And then he came back in. "This doesn't work," he said. So I replaced it with another copy. Again he left and then came back.

"Same thing," he said, nicely, almost apologetically.

"It doesn't work in your car?"

"Yeah."

"Weird. Show me?" He nodded. It was a slow night so I told my co-worker I'd be right back, and this young, dark-haired man led me out to the gritty strip mall parking lot. We walked across the pavement and over to a Ford Mustang with California plates. I think it was blue. Inside it smelled of warm leather. He put the key in and turned to draw on the battery, opened the Mellencamp CD case, and slid the disc into a discreet slot in the dash. The machine sputtered a moment and then a screen delivered a flashing error message.

"Same as the last one," he said.

"Huh." I think, by this point, I had begun to wonder if he was a ballplayer, tipped by some combination of the voice, the car, and maybe his physique, though I remember him then looking as he later did in the majors, slump-shouldered and unimposing. But I must have suspected it; that's the only explanation I can come up with now for why the next thing out of my mouth was, "Do you mind if I ask what you're doing in Ottawa?"

He looked around then and he saw what I saw, only I expect he saw it differently. We were standing in the parking lot of a strip mall on a commercial road lined with fast food spots and characterless office buildings, an industrial park to the west and, to the east a few clicks, the suburban neighbourhood where I'd grown up. The building behind us housed a Lebanese bakery, a window blind outlet, a wig shop, a U-frame-it place, and a pancake restaurant in addition to the CD store where I worked. The parked cars were all nosed out toward St. Laurent Blvd. If you were to drive north on it for three kilometres or so, past the city bus depot, past the strip club, past the dental offices and discount medical supply stores, the mattress mart, and the big mall, then hang a left on Coventry Road, you'd be at Lilly's place of employment, Ottawa Stadium, where sparse crowds shiver out Triple-A baseball games in April and May, then sweat through the summer until Labour Day marks the end of the season. Ten thousand fans used to pack the park each night but over the years most of them had come to refocus their attention elsewhere, most notably on the NHL's Senators, whose annual playoff runs impinge on the baseball season.

"I'm playing baseball," he said, "for the Lynx."

"What's your name?"

"Ted Lilly," he said.

"No shit," I said. "I saw you pitch last week."

"Yeah?"

"Yeah."

"You go to a lot of the games?" he asked.

"As many as I can. Usually with my dad. But I'm here a lot," I said, pointing back at the store.

"Can I ask you something?"

"Yeah."

"How come more people don't come?"

Ted Lilly damn near broke my heart and all I could do was give him his money back and apologize for whatever manufacturing defect had prevented him from blasting "Jack & Diane" on the way to his next start.

Thereafter, I saw him pitch a couple of times in person and a bunch on TV. He played 15 major league seasons, took a couple of no-hitters deep into games, tussled with Toronto manager John Gibbons, gave up his share of home runs, and retired from the game in 2013. In all he struck out 1,681 big league hitters, won 130 games and lost 113, and posted a career ERA of 4.14. In the strange economy of baseball, those are his numbers.

My own performance is harder to tally. I can say that even without hard numbers, the day I met Ted Lilly I knew in my heart that my effort and drive were both below the Mendoza Line. I routinely grounded into double plays, and I was in the habit of leaving runners on base. I would be no one's draft pick.

Ted Lilly's question to me deserved an answer bound up in Ottawa's identity, a city declared boring by visitors and locals alike, a place where, as the expression has it, they roll up the sidewalks after dark. It's a town full of bureaucrats, I was always told. And if there was one thing the locals hated more than being reminded of any of that, it was being compared to Toronto, home to the Jays and Leafs, an undeniably big league town four hours down the highway. Ottawa? Well, they had the Lynx, and there's a part of the city's makeup that resented being designated a minor league town, even if that's what the demographics suggested. Toronto remained Toronto, even as Ottawa grew moderately more cosmopolitan.

The Lynx debuted in 1993 and in the early going the team coasted on novelty (professional baseball in Ottawa!), then success (1995 Governor's Cup champions!). Both quickly receded, however, and the team became a reminder of the city's place in the second tier. In comparison the Senators, who'd played their first game in 1992, spoke to something flashier and more upscale: a steakhouse in a suburban hockey arena, hostesses in black clothing, valet parking, hundred dollar tickets. The Lynx were cheap seats, cardboardy french fries, and an old mesh Tim Raines jersey. They were comfortable, not aspirational, a minor league baseball team in a city in love with hockey. As Ottawa attempted to complete its transition from a logging town, where the mix of rough-hewn characters and rocky Eastern Ontario stodginess chafed like a wool collar, to its mid-century incarnation as a prim and secure government centre, and on to twenty-first century world capital, the Lynx fell out of favour as an entertainment choice. By the late 1990s Ottawa no longer wanted to think of itself as a minor league town. In some ways the Lynx had come along at precisely the wrong time and their tenure was always doomed.

That's what I could have told Ted Lilly, had I the time, were we not standing in a parking lot in the waning daylight, if he'd wanted the whole truth. But I don't believe it honestly mattered to him, in the end. He was a ballplayer, on his way through, and he'd soon find himself elsewhere.

I had no idea where I'd find myself. How we conceive of and define ourselves, the weight those notions carry, the way they're informed by how we define success, these are all fluid things, hard to pin down from one day to the next. But I know that when Ted Lilly and I lived, briefly, in the same city, I was busy perfecting self-castigation while he worked on his hook. He fooled hitters and I fooled no one. He was pitching and I wanted to write.

Already a dropout of several post-secondary programs, adrift and clueless, I had by that time forgotten that in order to be a writer one had to actually write. Instead I was staying up all night listening to moody post-bop albums, reading the classics, and growing gloomier by the day. Mine was a muggy existence, ideas pouring from my brow like humidity, but I lacked the wherewithal to do anything with them, or maybe just the belief that I could. Likeliest of all is that I was afraid that attempting to do so—i.e., striving—would involve interacting with people, and that prospect set off the whooping klaxons and shrieking horns of my social anxiety alarms. So I thought I'd bide my time, reasoning that such things ease with age, that my fears would abate with some practice.

When you're young you figure out a bit about who you are. Maybe you're clever and pretty good at doing something. Maybe that thing is throwing a ball, maybe it's writing stories. At some point you have to choose whether to coast on the skill you already have or invest in the work it'll take to keep getting better, because there comes a time when you're too old to be a prodigy anymore. Then you're just a person who might or might not do things, and without the work there won't be anything remarkable about you. That point came and went for me, and I was still sitting in the dark listening to Yo La Tengo.

By the time I figured all that out Ted Lilly was in the majors.

Success is a wavy and enigmatic thing. The scale slides. On February 1, success might be making the team out of Spring Training. On Opening Day, it might look like winning 20 games. By a cloudy afternoon in May it might just be getting out of an inning unscathed after you give up a leadoff triple.

I went back to school. I got a useless degree but I found a mentor. I moved in with the woman I'd later marry. We bought a house in the country. The roof leaked and we fixed it. I published a story. I got a ton of rejections and then I published another.

Now I have books to my name but you might still find me reading to six people in a tent at a literary festival, five of whom I know, one of whom is the host, and the microphone doesn't work so I'm being drowned out by the sound of traffic on the road immediately adjacent to the venue. Right now success is selling one or two books at that festival. It's getting the kids to bed before midnight. It's leaving the house most days despite all my urges to the contrary.

It's our limitations that make us what we are. Ted Lilly never threw 98 mph so he learned to place his pitches and he crafted a hell of a curveball. Social anxiety made me an observer and, as it turns out, observing is about 62 percent of writing, give or take.

By the time the Lynx played their final game in Ottawa Ted Lilly was in the first of three-and-a-half seasons with the Cubs. I got married, had a daughter, and was coming around to the opinion that Ottawa wasn't such a bad place, that any remaining ambivalence I held toward it had more to do with the ghost of the person I'd been there, the haunting after-image of all my own personal hangups, than anything inherent in my hometown's makeup. It was the psychic geography I'd laid over its physical features that made it such rough terrain for me.

And I'd learned a bit about what it means to work. Figured out "the best that I could do" is a statement of capability and intent. It meant that expending the most effort I could invest was the only way I'd get anything done. That nothing worth doing came easy and that there's always more work to do.

We're not all destined to be Cy Young winners. That doesn't mean we can't contribute or that we can't strike out 1,681 major league batters or that we never pick up a ball to begin with. It means we pass through the world collecting awareness of ourselves, both what we are and what we aren't. It means putting that awareness to good use. It means working harder.

I expect Ted Lilly came to know all this, if he didn't already know it when our lives momentarily intersected.

Picture us there: a Californian southpaw and a would-be writer working in a music store. He just wanted to hear "Pink Houses" but some encoding error or manufacturing slip-up got in the way. I wanted to help him but I couldn't. It was beyond me then.

LOST IN THE FOG

Up on the north side at Wrigley they got the game in without a delay, but it was soupy. On the south side the Sox and Jays, a pair of teams that appeared lost in the fog at several intervals during the early part of the 2013 season, watched as a heavy grey mist rolled off Lake Michigan and enshrouded U.S. Cellular Field. From the broadcast booth you couldn't see the outfielders.

The umpiring crew convened, discussed, and called for a delay. The players left the field, some jogging, some strolling. Toronto starter R.A. Dickey looked like a peripatetic as he left the mound and engaged catcher Josh Thole in conversation en route to the dugout.

The paying customers at U.S. Cellular settled in, pulled out stadium blankets, or headed for the concessions. Some doubtless watched games in other cities on their phones while they waited for theirs to resume. Some went home.

Those of us watching on TV were shuttled over to another broadcast, another city, another pair of teams. The crawl along the bottom of the screen said the Jays game was DELAYED DUE TO FOG. So we waited. Better than an hour in all. We waited.

As a concept, the delay is a strange thing. I've been thinking about this. It serves as a handy encapsulation of our relationship to this game. Because what other sport treats us to this?

Why do we submit to it? Things aren't quite right just now, it says. Bear with us here while we wait for this storm to pass and then we'll get back to the game. Maybe.

In Chicago the Jays were hungover from an exhausting weekend series with Texas, including an 18-inning win on Saturday and a sunny packed-house Sunday in which they very nearly came from behind, and so probably didn't mind sitting an extra hour. Or, given that it pushed back the end of the game, maybe they did. I once sat in the dugout during a rain delay at a Triple-A game in Ottawa and the players, I can tell you, were not eager to get back out on the field. "Call the game," they kept saying. "Just call the damn game."

The fog rolled off Lake Michigan, high up among the stanchions before settling on the field like a dropped handkerchief, and there was no question of playing. It was impossible. The prospect of balls dropping from the sky unseen and doing outfielders some harm was real. The rules state that the game must be delayed if the weather or some other factor (such as, say, bees) presents a danger to the players. The fog did just that, so in came the players and out went the tarp. And when we, sitting at home before our TVs, said to ourselves, "I will wait," it revealed something of who we are and why baseball is our game.

We carry to baseball some desire for clemency, some wish to lay ourselves down before it, to know that it is bigger than us. A willingness to submit to its whims. In truth, in the height of summer when we begin to speak in terms of "races" and "going down the stretch" we are perfectly willing to be swallowed by it. It is, in some respects, the penitent's sport. Its losing streaks and slumps, its prolonged displays of futility even among the very best players and teams, test the hardiest among us. Often my sense at season's end, after the last out of the Series has been recorded, is one of extreme longevity. Can anyone actually remember April?

We are lost in it. The world is obscured by baseball's blinding fog. Or is it life outside of baseball that obscures a true thing?

Look at it as a weather event, an explainable natural phenomenon, but look at the fog also as a thing of queer beauty. How lacy and delicate, this curtain of floating water lowered over a baseball stadium, cloaking the lights, the upper deck, blanketing the soft green grass. See how it evokes apparitions and spectres, maybe even brings to mind an enchanted cornfield in remotest Iowa and the players disappearing within it.

Here's what that wispy and nebulous interruption at U.S. Cellular suggested to me: baseball is the name we give to a covert belief in magic. It's what we call the yearning, the desperate, clawing need for something pregnant with the impossible. It reminded me of what a strange game baseball is—one that can be delayed by snow, by rain, by fog, by swarming insects. One that delivers more frustration than joy, but thereby engenders hope of a most stubborn and browbeaten variety.

Given all of this it occurs to me that what baseball requires of us is not mere attention, not understanding, not analysis, but belief. Belief in something that rolls on whether we heed it or not, and that is capable of punishing us, of bruising our hearts when we do pay attention, but which also stands to issue great rewards when attention transmogrifies into faith. And how, finally, is that belief measured? In what units? Number of prayers lobbed heavenward? Is it perhaps measurable in a person's willingness to sit through a delay? In the number of hours spent waiting, unsure even that the game will resume at all? We can only be who we are. That's what occurred to me when news came that the Jays-Sox game would momentarily resume. That I had waited over an hour for the resumption of what was—let's face it—a fairly insignificant game in early June. That I had not switched the channel to hockey, because hockey does not move me nearly so much. That I had not turned the TV off and moved on because I recognize my need for baseball, for the ritual it provides, on hot nights in June or chilly ones in October. It is, I thought, a belief beyond my control, to which I willingly submit.

Dickey retook the mound and went on to get tagged for a bunch of runs. The Jays lost 10–6 and that was it. That was what I'd stayed up to watch, what I'd waited for. The sting wasn't salved until the next night when a ninth-inning dinger by José Bautista gave Toronto a chance to steal a victory in extras.

Was that enough? Was that enough to justify belief? A fog delay followed by a loss followed the next day by an improbable win? No. That's not what sows belief. It's something longer than that. A season of delays and losses, sprinkled with wins. Ten such seasons. Twenty. And the hope that it will all turn around next year. Or the next. It's understandable, given all this, that one might ask: all this loss and frustration and fruitless attention—is it enough to sustain us? But one must never be surprised by the response.

MADISON BUMGARNER
AND THE BEAUTIFUL LIE

In his article naming the big lefty the 2014 Sportsman of the Year, *Sports Illustrated*'s Tom Verducci recounted a story from Spring Training in Scottsdale, Arizona wherein Madison Bumgarner and his wife Ali—described as "an expert field dresser"—were making use of an off-day from the Giants' camp to rope cattle (stay with me here) when Bumgarner saw what he took to be a rattlesnake. He attacked the thing with an axe, as anyone would; if you've no axe within arm's reach you really have no business calling yourself an outdoorsman. The snake thus dispatched, Ali took a closer look and found two baby bunnies inside the serpent's stomach, one of which was still alive.

The Bumgarners, naturally, nursed the rabbit to health and when the time was right they released it back into the wild. This, we can agree, is a hell of a story even if it's only partially true. In the face of such a perfectly engineered tale the amount of truth is, finally, incidental, barely even cosmetic. But in this story is nestled all the beautiful little characteristics of a certain breed of Perfect American Hero: self-reliant, resourceful, savage, but also caring. Davy Crockett on four days' rest. Paul Bunyan with a baseball glove, only in that glove this Bunyan had a little baby bunny! Which he rescued from a rattlesnake's belly and nursed back to health.

Madison Bumgarner doesn't need this, of course. He is the author of arguably the greatest World Series pitching performance of all time and that is enough. That he is the subject of bunny-related legends too makes him only the latest locus of a heady desire—call it a yearning—to graft onto baseball all the things America loves about itself. There is violence and love, one piggybacking the other. There is a gunslinging creation myth and the pull of the Frontier.

A sizable portion of America persists in the belief that the country's heart is still more rural than urban. Baseball fits within this belief and it's easy to will all sorts of sentimental pastoralities on the impeccable green diamonds situated in the midst of post-industrial cities of glass and concrete and soured hope. The longing for a connection between the game and a bucolic past goes back some ways; it was already a very real impulse by the turn of the last century, when the Mills Commission was convened to come up with baseball's origin story and settled on the malarkey of Abner Doubleday inventing it in a pasture outside of Cooperstown, New York. That location—picturesque, unspoiled, and in the heart of leatherstocking country in upstate New York—and the character of Doubleday—a Civil War hero and native son —were both overdetermined and perfectly chosen. So much so that not even the documented fact that Doubleday was nowhere near Cooperstown in the summer of 1839 when he was said to have invented the game could dispel the myth.

The Cooperstown story caught on though and in 1939 they stuck the Hall of Fame there. Every year thousands of fans, retired players, and media types converge on a scenic small town—hard by the shores of idyllic Otsego Lake and snuggled in the lap of the verdant Catskill Mountains—and spend a pretty, homespun weekend polishing that legend.

We know it's not true. We know the sport evolved from the English game of rounders and its many variants played in towns and cities and pastures across the United States. We know that what we recognize as baseball today was codified by Doc Adams, president of the New York Knickerbockers club, at a convention in January 1857. We know, too, that New York then was so devoid of green space that the Knickerbockers had to go across the river to Elysian Fields in Hoboken, New Jersey to find room to play. But still, Cooperstown is lovely.

Bumgarner too is alluring in the way of unspoiled things. If sport is proxy war Bumgarner is the Republic's folksy Cincinnatus, toiling through the summer and into the fall to assure victory, then returning to anonymity on his land in the hills of North Carolina to spend the winter tending his livestock. The narrative around Madison Bumgarner hinges on notions of manliness, rough-edged and guided by a stern but fair moral code, coughing up imagined nostalgia for some gloried time of yore when men were men and women knew how to clean a fresh kill. That's not America today; the average major leaguer is just as likely to be from Miami or suburban Dallas, or San Pedro de Macorís, or Kyoto. The story sticks all the same.

The narrative surrounding the North Carolinian is appropriately hagiographic; Bumgarner is easily idealized because the idea for which he stands is a simple one. But there's a touch of malice in such myth building, too, and something sour in marvelling at a man's apparent simplicity. This also has a long history in baseball. Rube Waddell's nickname was not bestowed affectionately, and Ring Lardner's busher stories about fictional pitcher Jack Keefe of Bedford, Indiana were a conduit for cityfolk like Lardner to both celebrate and ridicule rural Americans.

The common thread among these narratives is the expression of a yearning for a long-lost paradise, but at a a cynical remove. It's urban sophistication with a dose of suspicion; a self-hating, comfortable middle class. There's a strain too of the anti-intellectualism that's present in so much American rhetoric, both then and now. In that sense Bumgarner is the current embodiment of a protean American fantasy, a durable but malleable frontier narrative retailored over generations to remain stylish but always cut from the same fabric.

That both the example of Rube Waddell and the stories of Ring Lardner recall the indentured servitude of the reserve clause era—a time when ballplayers were seen as and treated like zoo specimens rather than people, let alone autonomous labourers—is not without relevance to the way in which we are sold Madison Bumgarner, World Series MVP. He's a freak, we are told, not only for the way he performs (by the end of 2014 his World Series ERA stood at a microscopic 0.25) but for the manner in which he eschews the trappings of his success. He doesn't appear to care much at all for his millions. He doesn't drive a Lamborghini or empty bottles of Grey Goose with supermodels in a VIP room. He is, in the parlance, a throwback, rough hewn, modest, independent, stoic. "Good," we say, "more athletes ought to be like him," a sentiment that carries a whiff of what we might daintily term racial exceptionalism; it's worth remembering that whatever his attitude toward his riches, he's due to earn $12 million in the last guaranteed year of his current contract.

Everyone requires a little self-delusion to get by. That's true whether you're a single person or a nation of 318 million people. As self-serving myths go, the one that has grown up around Madison Bumgarner is largely benign. For his part, the pitcher doesn't appear to have any intentional hand in the narrative's creation; he doesn't appear to care much about this sort of thing at all. He reads authentic, even as the storylines enveloping him shade into the baroque. Anything that surrounds him, any hopes pinned on him, any grand ideas for which he is assumed to stand, are our responsibility, not his. The parts of Madison Bumgarner's persona that are real are of his own creation. It's the parts made up by us, up here in the cheap seats, or watching from home, that should be viewed with some suspicion.

JOY IN ABEYANCE AND THE STUBBORN PERSISTENCE OF HOPE

I'm sorry to report that as we age we tax our ability to believe in perfect things. We learn the folly of making heroes of human beings. The twilight of hope seeps in as the years mount; joy can prove harder to come by and easier to distrust. People have a way of being something other than exactly what we need them to be. I'm only the messenger here, as dismayed as you are by this truth but determined to call it as I've seen it: stubbornly, people remain people, which is to say human, with all the fallibility the word implies.

Given enough time I think nearly everyone comes to realize this. The lucky among us avoid having it happen all at once in a sudden trauma when an idol steps wrong, but rather through a casual egress, myriad instances of mild disillusionment gradually draining the reserves of hope. This is the best-case scenario, maybe, preferable even to maintaining a pollyannish naivety.

Never meet your heroes, we're advised, and this is true of athletes as well as artists, actors, elected officials, thinkers, first responders. It's not worth the letdown. Better yet, don't raise them up to begin with.

But maybe it's unavoidable to make heroes of ballplayers. I'm certainly prone. A buzzy, addictive sort of excitement occurs when a blurring kinesis produces the desired outcome—a run or an out. I watch baseball in the hope of seeing something perfect and I have seen rare, perfect things: Ozzie Smith's defense, José Bautista's home run in the seventh inning of the 2015 ALDS, Cal Ripken's everyday commitment, the 2004 Boston Red Sox.

When such amazing things happen, the most convenient tag to hang on the actors is "hero," though it is itself a vague, compromised, misleading, and baggage-laden term. Ballplayers aren't superhuman, but in isolated moments they're about the closest thing we've got. Mike Trout climbing a wall to steal a home run bears only the most superficial resemblance to the people I encounter on a daily basis. When I watch the speed with which Bryce Harper swings a bat I'm tempted to look at my hands and say, "They can *do* that?"

Here's the rub, though: we too quickly assign greatness to those capable of handling a fastball or picking a sinking line drive off their shoetops. "Great things are done by great people," whispers the simplest, most binary precinct of the brain—or the heart. But ballplayers don't lessen suffering. They don't feed the hungry or cure the sick. They don't craft policy. They don't, in short, change the world in any measurable way.

Some of them are, in fact, bad people. Time and again we're reminded of this. Yet my childish inclination remains to believe, or wish, that among those who are routinely capable of on-field brilliance there are specimens who would prove to be exemplary human beings in all aspects of life. Despite the knowledge I've accumulated, the disappointments suffered, I still want heroes. And I still want my kids to have heroes too.

I can't think of any player more deserving of the mantle than Roberto Clemente. I never saw Clemente play; he died three-and-a-half years before I was born when the plane he'd chartered to bring supplies to Nicaraguan earthquake victims fell into the sea off San Juan, Puerto Rico. His final hit was his 3,000th. The Hall of Fame waived the five-year waiting period and inducted him into Cooperstown the following summer. He's an ideal: the rare combination of aesthetic sublimity, statistical achievement, principled action, and personal grace. He is among the most uncomplicated of heroes. He offers no downside, only dignity and faultless comportment. He's a resoundingly admirable human being, laudable top to bottom. There are no apparent pills to swallow. And I wish he were around now, for me to watch and for my daughter to hold up high.

Months before our girl was born my wife and I went to Chicago. I'd never been to Wrigley Field before. It was a cold, drizzly afternoon in April and the Brewers ended up shelling the Cubs. I bought a jersey and a cap, had a beer and a dog, glanced at my wife's pregnant belly and experienced the litany of hopes that all baseball-loving expectant parents do: that my kid would have the chance to experience all this, that she'd love it as much as I do, that she'd select heroes for herself— hopefully ones as commendable as Clemente—to exalt in their victories and die a little with their defeats.

Daughters come into a world that will prove hostile to them. I'm not telling you anything you don't already know. Life is chock full of dangers for all of us, but if we're being honest we must admit that it's going to be more treacherous for our daughters than for our sons. That our daughters will contend with legislators who view women's bodies as property, and women not as individual human beings but as a contiguous mass, a vast, rhetorical battleground. That they will be expected to give more effort for less pay, and face workplace pressures unknown or misunderstood by men. That they will live with sickening, routine, daily fear of a sort that our sons will not even vaguely comprehend. We have to admit that they will become women in a world bent on punishing them for that simple fact, and determined to deny them agency at every turn. And heaven help our daughters if they ever venture onto the Internet.

The world is too much. It encourages retreat, or at least it does in me. It makes me run to places of solace. And there are none more important to me than the ballpark, or failing that, a couch before a TV showing a game from somewhere. Anywhere. Maybe that makes me simple. Perhaps it suggests I'm lost. Regardless, I turned to baseball in even greater earnestness after my daughter was born both to distract me from my own worry and to have something to show her. I wanted, in addition to that sense of safety and the beautiful arcana of the game, to give her heroes. I'd be happy, of course, if she made heroes of Alice Munro and Kim Gordon and Maryam Monsef, our local Member of Parliament—the first Afghan-born Canadian ever elected to Parliament. But I wanted to offer her this safe place, this open ground, and, hopefully, heroes to admire. Physical elegance, moments of high drama, something to talk about with strangers. A rooting interest but also a sense of calm, an implicit belief that once through the turnstile a place can be devoted to something so perfect and can, as a result, grant refuge, if only for an afternoon or a warm summer evening. A ballpark as a place to bring her tremulous heart when it's wounded, a place that suggests the miraculous is attainable merely by virtue of the game played on its well-tended surface, a game that so often inspires men to be their best selves—where they are, in short, heroic.

Maybe to her it'll always be just a game, a sport, and not a trembling holy thing like it is for me. Perhaps she'll find the gender politics of the thing troubling, be put off by the stranglehold on the conversation surrounding the game held by a small group of likeminded white men. Perhaps she'll decide not to invest the ceaseless energy required to defend her fandom against those who'd want to challenge it because it doesn't look exactly like theirs. I couldn't fault her for any of that.

But I take her to games just in case. Sit with her and cheer. Explain what I can, answer her questions. Show her what I love about it—and the players I love most—and hope that it washes over her the way it does me. I won't try to force it because it can't be forced. But I will hope fervently that something about baseball captures her so that she has this sport and these heroes to share with me always. On the other hand, if she rejects it, if she finds no heroes there, I can comfort myself with the knowledge that she had the choice. I can say to myself, well, at least I offered it. At least I showed her the good things these ballplayers are capable of doing, the people they can be. At least I took her to a game or two.

In her presence it has become harder to pass off the messier things men may tend to do off the diamond. I won't lie to her about it; I am held to the account of her moral development. It might be easy to celebrate the actions of a person like Dock Ellis, who threw a no-hitter while on acid, who spoke truth to power on matters of race and class, who waited five years to plunk Reggie Jackson after Jackson hit an Ellis pitch over the roof of Tiger Stadium in the '71 All-Star Game, who overcame addiction to become an addiction counselor after retiring from baseball, and who collaborated with poet Donald Hall on a book. But once I heard that Dock Ellis hit his wife the deal was off. He was stricken from the hero list. People are complicated but children don't traffic in nuance and in such instances—when in search of heroes—neither should we.

Time and again: DUIs, domestic violence, the use of performance-enhancing drugs, racism, misogyny, homophobia. A complete list of the ways in which our heroes let us down would be as long as it is dispiriting.

One of my childhood heroes was Ken Griffey, Jr., and I bring him up as an example of the myriad ways that heroes can break your heart. If a legitimate scandal exists that implicates Junior I don't know it and I don't wish to. But it was his humanness that undid him: the body failed. He was All-World for the first half of his career, those initial 11 years he spent with the Mariners, but he was a puzzle for the last half, after he'd asked for and received a trade to his hometown Reds. It was a slow, painful fade, hard to watch and impossible not to wish to see turned around. But the thing that made him so exciting to watch never came back, and for better than a decade holding Junior as your hero meant looking back at what he'd once done or imagining the records he should have broken had he not been hurt, though he was still technically an active player.

So much fallible humanity can dent the soul. But it's also what makes worthwhile all this thought and emotional vulnerability and the time you'll spend caring about baseball. When things go right the heroes will show you what we're capable of as athletes, citizens, and human beings. Once you make your peace with the fact that you're likely going to wind up cheering for a team that is, legally speaking, a subsidiary of a multinational corporation—as storied as your team might seem, as hallowed and cherished as they are to you, to the board of directors they're just another holding—you're going to be left with the faces of the people wearing the uniforms and swinging the bats. They'll do impressive things, win big games, amass noteworthy numbers. But they're ultimately human and they'll do human things too. They will occasionally falter. They'll strike out with the tying run on third. They'll refuse a child an autograph. They'll hold contemptible views and express them publicly. They'll issue statements through lawyers. They'll turn themselves in. They'll go to trial. The punishments they receive from the Commissioner will seem paltry. Their endorsement deals will survive. These men will skate by materially unaffected by their mistakes. And all of it, though never totally unexpected, will still hurt you. Give people a chance and likely as not they'll break your heart.

Cynicism is the natural response, but baseball also tends to resist jadedness because it so routinely allows glimpses of magic—the nonchalant inclusion of the impossible amid the workaday—so if there's a venue appropriate to the creation of heroes it's the ballpark. Still, the bad things will happen and the disappointment will mount. It's a sure thing. So why make heroes of any of them?

Though few, they are there, the ones deserving of faith. Clemente embodied the rarest of combinations; his is a lofty example. You could go a lifetime without finding another like him. As soon as Barry Bonds became the all-time home run king I hoped for another to surpass him in short order not because I think Bonds was an evil man for doing what he did but because I wanted my kids to know an uncomplicated hero, someone whose actions didn't need to be explained away or placed into a nuanced context.

I've had this argument with myself, considered doing away with my belief in heroes in the interest of eliminating the frustration, the letdown, the inevitable moment of disappointment. But I can't. The game's appeal lies in what's possible, not what's likely, and I don't think you can love it without some residual belief in heroes. And you can't know all the joy it has to offer unless you put your heart on the line. Ultimately, I tell myself, to believe in heroes is to persist in the equally stubborn belief that people can show us something better, and I don't want to let go of that.

BIRTH OF A RIGHT FIELDER

Just as it always does, the sky over Dodger Stadium yawned like a lap steel guitar, a showy wash of SoCal pinks and oranges. And just as he always does, Vin Scully sat in the booth and invited you into his parlour to listen to him tell you about the Dodgers in his perfect, mannered, mid-century American voice.

The Padres were in town, making the short trip up the I-5 to tangle with their division mates. The Dodgers, it so happened, were the only thing keeping San Diego out of last place and the Friars sought to take three from LA in order to further stuff that cushion.

There was a void in LA's sporting heart in the summer of 2013. The NBA playoffs rolled on without the Lakers or Clippers and there had been little to cheer on the diamond as both the Angels and Dodgers had disappointed in the early going. The pre-season prognosticators had agreed the Dodgers would contend, maybe even walk away with the West. But by the first of June, in last place and seven-and-a-half games back, Angelenos were calling for manager Don Mattingly's head. Donnie Baseball, the reasoning went, had been given all the pieces. So why wasn't he winning?

By the time the lineup cards were exchanged on that Monday evening, a new tool had appeared in the Dodgers' shed: Yasiel Puig, from Cienfuegos, who'd passed through Mexico, Rancho Cucamonga, and Chattanooga on his way to Los Angeles. Touted for his bat, the Dodgers brought the outfielder up from Double-A to kickstart their sluggish offense. It was an undeniably desperate move. But the team's brass knew that, though desperation almost never pays off, every so often it does.

So when the Dodgers rushed from the dugout and onto the field in the top of the first in their brilliant home whites, with blue accents and the incongruous red numbers on the left side of the torso which, like Scully, go all the way back to Brooklyn, they did so with Puig among their ranks. And Puig sprinted straight out to right field.

What is it about right fielders? They have always been my favourites. How to explain that? Their speed, perhaps. Their arms, of course. A howitzer for an arm is a prerequisite for the job. Think of Clemente. Ichiro. Dave Parker. Vladimir Guerrero. Something about the spacing contributes too, the geography, the layout of the game—or is that my imagination? The right fielder seems distant, the occupier of his own island out there, separate and watchful. He stands with his throwing arm hanging loose by his side in the hopes of putting it to use. The sac fly. The runner foolishly attempting to score from first. The right fielder seems to exist only for those moments. A quiet weapon kept under lock until required. Until the moment he is cocked and unloaded.

There is no uniform build among right fielders. Think of lanky Guerrero, early on, all impossibly long limbs. Think of small, wiry Ichiro or big Dave Parker. Clemente, hard and lean. Puig is thick, broad-shouldered and stands six foot three. His arms are enormous. He looks like a power hitter. Like a DH.

Defense isn't measured as easily as offense, of course, despite our efforts to quantify it. The scouting reports said Puig could play right, had the tools, possessed speed and instinct. They put him in right, but they could just as easily have put him in left. The position was beside the point. The Dodgers wanted his bat.

A good crowd packed Dodger Stadium, or a halfway decent one, anyway: 37,000-plus. In most parks that's a full house. Dodger Stadium, of course, is the largest ballpark there is, with room for 56,000, so it looked a bit empty on the night of Puig's debut. Still, for a Monday night game between a couple of bottom-dwellers it was a respectable crowd. The people of Los Angeles, tickets in their pockets, lawyers and gardeners, actors, janitors. From Palo Alto and Burbank and Nuevo Laredo and San Salvador. Native sons and daughters, immigrants, refugees.

There is something of the refugee about the stadium too. The Dodgers were refugees from Brooklyn. Pushed out, as their owner saw it, by an inability to shoehorn modernity into a hardscrabble borough, and so seeking a new place and finding it in California. And in placing their new stadium in Chavez Ravine, the city and the team created new refugees, using eminent domain clauses to bum-rush the locals—Mexican-Americans for the most part—telling them it was for new housing developments and then building a ballyard instead. They levelled a hill and filled in the ravine so Sandy Koufax could set to work.

And now Puig himself, a defector, and a refugee too if you consider it a universal right to ply your trade in the major leagues, a right denied him by Cuban authorities. So he slipped out, crossed the Gulf, established residency in Mexico and waited for the big leagues to call. Before long, the Dodgers did.

Yasiel Puig, those displaced Angelenos, the Dodgers; maybe, in some manner, we are all in search of refuge.

His first two major league hits already logged, Puig sprinted and danced back out to right, glove on his hand, in the top of the ninth. It was 2–1 Dodgers. With one out and the Padres' Chris Denorfia on first, Dodgers closer Brandon League was two outs away from sealing the win.

All of the great throws: Ichiro gunning down Terrence Long at third. Bo Jackson from the warning track in left. What ties them together is the sense that we've witnessed some quiet, subtle violation of the natural laws that govern us all. Gravity and speed and distance. A ball that travels too far, too quickly, hits its target too perfectly. A bang-bang play. The runner's face betraying disbelief.

All the throws, and another possible at any moment. These are the big leagues and every player in uniform on these fields is capable of something remarkable, some transcendent moment of greatness. The truly great throws have so often come from right field. But a kid in his first game? Too much to ask.

There Puig stood in right field, slack and rhythmic. His right arm hung there, swayed a bit. Denorfia on first, one out, and Padres left fielder Kyle Blanks stood in. A ball and two strikes. From the stretch, League threw low and away, Denorfia took off on the pitch. Blanks hacked at the ball and skied it to right. There was a catch in the collective breath of the Dodgers faithful as they watched the ball climb into the darkening SoCal night.

Puig twisted and turned toward the wall, an inefficient backwards path, before camping under it, his glove flexed and ready. Already, it seemed, before he'd even caught the ball, he eyed Denorfia who, with too great an air of casualness, was over near second. The moment—the very instant—the ball settled into Puig's glove, the atmosphere of Dodger Stadium changed.

Torso pointed toward the infield, legs somewhat splayed, Puig reared back and fired the ball to first. This kid, this rookie, this Cuban defector with big numbers and an avalanche of hype, had the crazy idea that he might double off Denorfia, out there in no man's land, and end the game. Hubristic, ludicrous, a bit cocksure? Yes, all of those things.

And the throw was perfect. Perfect. Flat-footed, from the warning track, with no windup, no chance to set his feet, he threw a perfect strike. Adrian Gonzalez, manning first for LA, seemed surprised, but extended his glove out to the exact spot where Puig's laser beam needed to be. Bang-bang. The home plate umpire, covering the play, hesitated, perhaps ensuring he'd in fact seen what he thought he'd seen: Yasiel Puig, in his first major league game, doubling off the runner at first with an impossible throw from the warning track. Yes, he decided. It really happened. A double play. Second and third outs recorded. Dodgers win.

Beautiful things began happening thereafter in Chavez Ravine. The next night against the Padres, Puig hit two home runs and knocked in five in another win. Two nights after that he hit a grand slam against the Braves that left Vin Scully speechless. Through four games the right fielder had nine RBIs. It's hard to imagine living in LA and not being completely absorbed by his early exploits.

The Dodgers needed his bat and he brought it. All the way from Chattanooga. From Cienfuegos. But for all his offensive acumen, for me it's that throw that lingers in the mind. That perfect throw. I add it to the list of greats: to Ichiro and Bo Jackson, to Ken Griffey, Jr., to Dave Parker. On the fly from the warning track, punishing Denorfia for his lackadaisical baserunning. A bullet, a guided missile, the right fielder winning the game, and so announcing himself: I'm here. By force of will, with great skill and enthusiasm, I'm *here*. On a Monday night in Dodger Stadium he arrived, the product of an apparently Athena-like birth, for all the mystery that had shrouded him. Suddenly, the Dodgers had a right fielder. Yasiel Puig—"The Wild Horse," Scully dubbed him—had found a kind of refuge, and so, in a sense, had we.

EVERYTHING IS BEAUTIFUL AND NOTHING MAKES SENSE

I don't know what it is about Toronto. I think about this from time to time and come up with nothing bankable. I usually arrive at something not entirely capturable by language— its *Toronto-ness*, finally, exasperatingly, its feel and vibration and smell and the speed and angle at which the wind comes off the lake. I'm not saying any of this is good or bad. It's both. It's neither. You grow up in Ottawa, four or five hours up the highway, a million psychological miles away, and you feel the gravity of a city like Toronto. You admire and resent it. You're not from there and you're acutely aware of that. You don't want to live there, and maybe more crucially you don't want to want to live there. Great place to visit, could never call it home, and so forth. But that doesn't really wrap up all the feelings and thoughts you have about the city; there are too many of them.

It's a place you've experienced so intimately and over such a long period of time that you can't unravel it all and see it as a city, a pixel on the world map, a locale. It's instead a disorganized mash of memories and faces and fears, bands you've seen, friends you've too often failed to call, games you've attended, couches on which you've crashed. It's a trick of light. It's a cold walk in autumn. It's a cab ride across town.

As Canadians we tend to undervalue ourselves, to deploy a kind of vacuum-packed modesty, so even Toronto— sprawling and cosmopolitan as it is—must conform to this self-effacement. After all, every single one of us knows someone who lives there. How could it be such a big deal? It's also the city most other global citizens associate with Canada, so it *must* be very Canadian. And if this is the case then it must be humble and unimpressive. That, crudely, is the consternating cognitive loop some/most/all of us on the outside have concerning Toronto. But it's not unimpressive. It's loud and vain and strange and mutable and cultured; it's quiet and meek and grey and unchanging and ignorant too. It's a lot of things at once. Mostly it's a screen, like all big cities: loci of desire and effort and failure and reinvention. Toronto's lack of focus is paradoxically its definition. It evinces a beautiful cultural jumble: roti up on Eglinton; a bored employee listening to dancehall while she closes up a Pizza Pizza location in North York; old Italian men waiting for a bus on Spadina; a veggie dog from a cart outside a lakeside concert venue; small bars; large parks; the lights at the end of the night; the long drive home.

This rambling about The Big Smoke all comes because I'm thinking of the Blue Jays as the *Toronto* Blue Jays and what that geographic qualifier actually means. The Blue Jays are, in addition to a collection of monetary interests based in Toronto and proof that Toronto is a Big League City, a civic symbol, an outward face of the town on the shores of Lake Ontario. They're the reason a fan in Kansas City, Missouri might have an opinion of the place. But I can't for the life of me figure out how the Blue Jays—or Toronto— appear or are interpreted by that woman in KC or, say, a baseball fan in San Diego or Baltimore. I can't penetrate that. I can't ever leave behind my associations in order to understand theirs, and the inaccessibility of that experience is baffling and confounding, but normal and absolute. This is lightweight thinking, pure Philosophy 101 stuff, but it was on my mind a lot during the late summer and into the fall of 2015 precisely because the US media said "Toronto" more in that span than they had in quite some time, Rob Ford's ugly mayoral tailspin notwithstanding.

The Blue Jays feel as homey and trusted and safe to me as Jerry Howarth's voice on my car radio as I drive the 401 between Kingston and Port Hope, or wend through cottage country, or take County Road 23 up toward Buckhorn. "The Blue Jays are in flight," he'll say when they score their first run, or "And there she goes!" when somebody hits one out, just as he's been saying on every radio and in every car I've owned for years and years and years. How can that experience—so familiar to me, so seemingly mine—jive with the experience of the untold millions out there who are also familiar with the team to whatever degree? This is some real epistemological sidetracking, I know. But how can the Blue Jays be so many things at once? How can Toronto be so many places at once? Are the Blue Jays inextricably an emblem of that city, and when I cheer for them am I just an outsider willing myself into their sphere? Is a Yankees fan in Havana who's never seen The Stadium still a Yankees fan or do they require some other designation?

If I've reached any sort of conclusion it's this: the Blue Jays are mine, but they're not mine. They're Toronto but they're also wherever I happen to be, and I love them and I resent them for all the suffering, and thank them for all the miracles, minor and major. It doesn't matter that I'm not a Torontonian. Fandom has no textbook, no manual. Nobody who suggests there's a right way to invest in a team is worth listening to. My connection, however tenuous, is decades old and involves memories of Jesse Barfield and Garth Iorg, but I could have hopped aboard the bandwagon during their latest playoff run and it wouldn't matter. Fandom isn't an exclusive club, it isn't a perk of paying taxes in a particular jurisdiction; it's only measured in a willingness to care.

In 2015 that caring had a long-sought emotional payoff. When the Jays front office splashed out at the trade deadline and picked up David Price, the biggest-name pitcher on the market at the time, I said to my dad on the phone, "It feels like when they got David Cone in '92, doesn't it?" Late that season Toronto sent young second baseman Jeff Kent and an outfielder named Ryan Thompson to the Mets for Cone. As with Price in 2015, it was the team's all-in moment, signalling to fans the ownership's belief that this was the year. It worked in '92, delivering a World Series title but also in roping the attention of a good number of Canadians, many of whom hadn't been watching baseball before that point.

Nothing guarantees anything, of course, least of all the acquisition of a starting pitcher, but maybe it tilts the odds a bit. Who knows. Cone pitched well in the late summer and through the autumn of 1992, but maybe more importantly his arrival goosed the energy around the team. The Blue Jays won the Series in six games and their celebration took place on the infield grass of Atlanta's Fulton County Stadium on October 24, 1992. It was a Saturday. I was 16 years old. I watched it with friends at a house in suburban Ottawa and afterward we went out into the street wearing our caps and sweatshirts. We had noisemakers. I don't know where we got them. We walked around and whooped and blew horns and clapped. A few cars recognized the cause of our stupidity and honked in solidarity. We were giddy with joy.

The late summer and fall of 2015 felt a lot like that. After the Jays treaded water for the first four months of the season most of us had counted the team out. It was odd then when GM Alex Anthopoulos flipped José Reyes for Troy Tulowitzki a few days ahead of the July 31 deadline. Odd, but great. Then Anthopoulos cashed in a horde of prospects for David Price.

The Price deal happened while I drove umpteen straight hours from Ontario to PEI, and I didn't hear about it until I emerged rumpled and bewildered from my Dodge Caravan at the other end. His first start took place a few days later and though the weather was absolutely perfect on the Island I skipped an afternoon at the beach to watch it on TV.

Toronto had just taken three of four from the American League-leading Royals, and were above .500 and climbing. The Twins were visiting. It was the civic holiday, the first Monday in August, and it was a summery afternoon, hot and bright. The roof was wide open, the stands full.

I don't know how many Blue Jays games I watched over the 20-plus years between their last World Series in 1993 and David Price's first start for them in August 2015. Certainly hundreds, possibly thousands. In that time, over all those games, I hadn't seen anything even remotely approaching the fervour and enthusiasm of that afternoon's crowd. Price dealt, the Jays scored, the fans lost their senses, and no one watching, either there or on television or a laptop or phone, in Regina or Iqaluit or Cavendish, PEI, could escape the impression that something pretty damned amazing was happening.

And so it went. August was long and hot and ecstatic; they won 21 games and lost just 6. There were 11 victories in a row, including a sweep of the first-place Yankees. The Jays assumed the top spot themselves on August 12. Their already torrential offense continued apace and the pitching improved. They'd spent the first four months of the season in the state of semi-anonymity in which they usually existed—largely ignored by the rest of the baseball world—but by the end of the month the Toronto Blue Jays were a headline. They were remarkable, so they were remarked upon. The story was compelling and everyone, it seemed, contributed to help it remain so. Russell Martin hit a big homer against New York; Edwin Encarnacion hit three as the Jays thumped the Tigers 15–1. September began in the same fashion: Ryan Goins hit a walk-off dinger in the bottom of the tenth to beat Cleveland. We watched Josh Donaldson (.297 AVG/.939 OPS/41 HR/123 RBI/122 R) put together his MVP season—something no Blue Jay had done since George Bell in 1987—strengthening his claim to the award nightly with barehanded bravado in the field, thunderous hitting, and baserunning that showed both great understanding of the discipline and a total disregard for his own physical well-being. The team clinched a playoff spot—their first in 22 years—on September 26 and secured the American League East four days later. And in the middle, Donaldson made sure that the Jays' last regular season home game was a happy memory, sending the Rays away with a second-deck shot in the bottom of the ninth of a tie game, his third walk-off home run of the year.

By then some 2.7 million people had gone through the turnstiles at the Rogers Centre, a number not seen since that last World Series. The Blue Jays were, in a way they hadn't been in almost a generation, everyone's shared interest, everyone's topic of conversation. They belonged once again to a whole country. Department stores stocked Jays gear. At my kids' school you couldn't tell the students apart; everyone was dressed the same, in blue T-shirts and caps. It was an amazing thing to see. Everywhere I wore my Jays hat someone was interested in talking about the team.

Late September took on its characteristic chill and October moved in. The Jays were to play the Rangers in the Division Series and it came as something of a shock to all of us that they had trouble with Texas. Pushed to a deciding fifth game, things were dire and drastic and strange and frightening until José Bautista stepped in to straighten it all out.

Bautista's home run in the seventh inning of that deciding game, and his subsequent bat flip, were watched— and celebrated—in ten provinces and two territories simultaneously. The moment was immediately iconic and at once about both the individual responsible and all of us witnessing it; it was for the overlooked. It was statement and declaration. It was Bautista's opportunity to transcend from steady fixture to legend. There are so few moments in baseball now, home runs especially, that succeed in breaking through the noise and the GIF churn and threaten to join moments like Bobby Thompson's pennant-winning shot in that timeless strata of epochal events. Bautista's did.

It wouldn't have been nearly as charged a moment though had it not come during that seventh inning. Even in looking over the game log I can't begin to make heads or tails of it. It unfurled with the liquid logic of a dream, making little sense in the moment, threatening at several points to tip into nightmare. In retrospect it's a river of flickering images seemingly unrelated to one another.

In 1908 the Giants lost the National League pennant when Fred Merkle failed to touch second base and was later forced out to end what should have been a New York victory. They called it "Merkle's Boner." In the top of the seventh of Game 5, Toronto catcher Russell Martin casually tossed a ball back to the pitcher only to have the ball glance off Ranger Shin-Soo Choo's bat and dribble up the third base line. Rougned Odor, on third, sprinted home even while the home plate ump waved time. Odor touched the plate, the sizable umpiring crew convened, had a chat with mission control in New York, and ruled the run legitimate. The Rangers were up by one and the Dome suddenly got ugly, debris raining onto the turf. It looked like a hockey game. John Gibbons lodged a protest and I gave some thought to writing an essay called "Martin's Boner."

But the Jays got out of that half inning, came up in the bottom of the seventh, and the Rangers forgot how to catch a ball. They booted three of them. With the bases loaded and nobody out, pinch runner Dalton Pompey was forced at home on a grounder to first by Ben Revere, but he took out catcher Chris Gimenez's legs, preventing a double play. The umpiring conference and review that followed might have caused a riot on Front Street had the umps not wisely and correctly ruled Pompey's slide legal. Donaldson hit a squeaker just over Odor's head, the tying run scored, and Bautista came up with runners on the corners.

That's the point at which the most vivid memory will begin, as the years pile up and we look back on the game. Just like a Jays fan need only say to another "Carter" and the whole "Touch 'em all, Joe" scene spools out in the mind, "Bautista" is now the call-word for unqualified joy, the water-in-the-desert feeling, the "Finally!" sensation that moment sparked in millions of us that night. For 22 years we had Joe Carter reaching for that Mitch Williams pitch, the ball slipping over the wall in left, Carter leaping and skipping as he made his way down toward first, the way he was lifted onto his teammates' shoulders when he arrived home.

That was matched by the memory of Bautista's murderous swing, the quick scowl, the toss of the bat high into the air. These became our new images and they can all be evoked by saying the man's name.

I lost it. My kids—watching with me at home—lost it. It was the most gloriously and deliriously deterministic moment imaginable. As unlikely as it was, it felt instantly inevitable, as though the whole strange, sad parade leading to it had made that home run inescapable, had written it in stone. It was, in the bent and furious rationale established by all that had occurred, the only appropriate outcome. It was fantasy made real, anti-logic captured on live TV. It was a bullet to the brain of objectivity. It made no sense whatsoever and it was beautiful.

What's perhaps just as amazing is that José Bautista had managed to make the city where he played likable to a nation that makes deriding it a sport of its own. Nobody had an ill word for Toronto in that moment—nobody in Canada, that is; I expect everyone in Texas did. Hell, there were even people in Montreal cheering for a team from Toronto. That's noteworthy.

Texas dispatched, Canada's team headed to Missouri to face the Royals in the ALCS. They dropped Games 1 and 2 by scores of 5–0 and 6–3. Then they headed back north.

Just as millions had spent two decades claiming to have been at the Carter game, everyone knew someone who had tickets to Games 3, 4, and 5 of the 2015 ALCS. They stuffed nearly 50,000 people into the Dome each of those nights and sealed it shut; by MLB's decree the roof was closed, though I remember those to have been decently temperate autumn days. The rest of us, coast to coast, behind insulated walls and double-hung windows, tuned in and prayed.

In Game 3 Tulowitzki, Donaldson, and Goins homered, and wunderkind Marcus Stroman did enough to earn the 11–8 win. Game 4 got ugly quick as Kansas City hung four runs on R.A. Dickey in the first. Things only got worse thereafter. Gibbons ended up bringing infielder Cliff Pennington in to pitch, which is all the summary you need. Final: 14–2 Royals, and the Jays were down three games to one.

Would you believe me if I said you could detect the deficit in people's posture? In Peterborough, some 130 kilometres from home plate, there was a slump in the populace's shoulders and I suspect the same to have been the case in towns all across the country. The local schoolyard was subdued. My son, who'd been wearing his Jays cap religiously since early September, questioned its theretofore presumed status as good luck charm. Across six time zones, Canadians likewise questioned their wardrobe choices.

Marco Estrada pitched masterfully to limit the Royals to one run on four hits in Game 5 and Toronto cruised to victory 7–1. Then it was back to Kansas City.

I was in a bar in Peterborough that night with friends, surrounded by people wearing blue jerseys, blue T-shirts, blue caps. I toted a talisman—a replica of a 1993 World Series ring encased in a cube of acrylic given to me years earlier. I placed it on the table around which we were gathered.

They hung in there; let the record say that for the Blue Jays. Bautista hit two big home runs; he was determined to do it all by himself if necessary. The rain came in the middle of the eighth. The 45-minute delay was a horrible torment but also a chance to sit and drink a while longer with friends. When play resumed the Royals took the lead 4–3. Russell Martin—from East York, Ontario—led off the ninth and singled, and then Dalton Pompey—from

Mississauga—came in as a pinch runner. Pompey stole second on the first pitch and third shortly thereafter. Kevin Pillar walked. These were the last spasms of hope. The tying run was on third base with none out. Dioner Navarro struck out but Pillar stole second. It was warm in the bar though the autumn wind blew outside. We huddled in close, played tabletops like drums, curled our hands into fists. There were people in British Columbia doing this. There were people in Newfoundland doing it.

Ben Revere struck out.

It was October 23. For nearly three full months we'd cheered a winning ballclub together. Tens of thousands of our friends and relations and fellow citizens attended those games, but millions more of us watched from afar. Collectively we loved something from Toronto. Close games, blowouts, a division clinched, we shared all of that, with each other and with the city. And then in the ninth inning of the sixth game of the American League Championship Series, with the tying run on third and the go-ahead on second, Josh Donaldson grounded out to Mike Moustakas at third and we all shared a great pain.

When the final out came—so long in coming but sudden as a coup de grâce—and the air went out of that bar, I looked around and realized that I was surrounded by people who felt, as I did, that they themselves had lost something. And of course we had. It's a rare and peculiar feeling, to rejoice so long and in such diffuse company. We'd just witnessed a season wherein it seemed that the Blue Jays could win in just about any implausible manner we might devise. If we could imagine it, they'd do it. And then it ended. It was, we all came to see at once, something that might not happen again before many or all of us were dead. It was that rare.

Then came the grief, the hard and indigestible feeling of a thing glimpsed but unattained. What awaited but winter in St. John's, winter in Brandon, winter in Toronto? The snow would fall on Yonge Street and it would be as cold and as drab and as lonely as any other part of the country. The long, dark months ahead would be full of what-ifs and if-onlys. The grief was geographically unbound on three sides, spreading west and north and east, but centred on Toronto, whose joy we'd taken as our own. And now we'd know its regret too. That's the deal. It's the risk you run when you invest. The cards are on the table and the ante is your heart.

But the tables were being cleared now, the servers swooping in to remove the glasses and pitchers and wing baskets, spent napkins and cutlery, scooping up handfuls of bills and coins, inserting cards into wireless handheld debit/credit machines. The imprecision of our exits was a further humiliation, now all suddenly inappropriately dressed in team wear we'd soon stash away.

With the game—and the season—over all we had in common was heartbreak, which is a lousy unifier. We filed out of that Peterborough bar just as people were filing out of bars all over the place, or turning off TVs or devices, seized by something like embarrassment for how publicly passionate we'd been, folding in on ourselves now, turning away. A dream had ended rudely, suddenly replaced with the grim exigencies of the barren months ahead. I wanted summer back. I wanted that feeling back. I wanted to say to those departing, "But what a season! What a thing they gave us all! How beautiful!" But no one was in the mood for it just then. The Blue Jays were ours to mourn that night, ours over which to keen and wail. Most preferred to mourn alone.

ICHIRO

He's shorter than I am, and wiry, not obviously muscular. He bends and stretches into odd arrangements of limb and core. There's no thunder about him, only light-footed élan. He doesn't swing for the fences; there's no resounding crack when a ball meets his bat. He's never looked the part of a great ballplayer, at least not of the classically American variety. He looks like something else entirely.

You've got your heroes and I've got mine. The statues in your pantheon might not match the ones in my temple, and we can sit around all day and argue about who deserves our adoration and who doesn't. You might try, for various reasons, to talk me out of Robbie Alomar (he spit on that ump, after all) or Ryne Sandberg (his abysmal managerial record looks like tarnish upon the gleaming trophy of his accomplishments), but you will not change my mind about Ichiro Suzuki.

I first saw him in August 2001. It was his first year in America after nine seasons in Japan, and he was on his way to both a Rookie of the Year award and an MVP nod. He was also the top All-Star vote getter. Ichiro was just kicking off what would turn out to be a 21-game hitting streak, one seemingly intended to silence his critics who, seizing upon a mini-slump following the All-Star break, were quick to brandish I-Told-You-So's regarding his small stature, his lack of major league experience, and his undeniable non-American-ness. On a steamy night in Seattle I watched him play right field against Toronto and collect a hit and a walk, and score a run in a losing effort. Not that the loss mattered; the Mariners had already won 83 games by that Thursday night, August 9th (that's not a typo), and they set an American League record with 116 wins for that incredible season, thanks in no small measure to Ichiro.

I was an instant fan. The Mariners became my second team after Toronto and I'd listen to their games on the Internet once Jays games had wrapped up. I followed Ichiro in the box scores and broke my personal rule to never get a current player's name on a jersey (they always get traded). Ichiro was an exception; he was my guy.

The reasons I adopted him so earnestly were many. His skill, certainly, but also his work ethic. His modest eccentricity. His dedication. On the field he was capable of incredible feats like The Throw, nailing Oakland's Terrence Long at third base with a bullet from right field that still looks as though some rule of physics was violated. The hitting streaks. That odd, asymmetric batting stance, and the manner in which he flung the bat out so that he was already three steps closer to first when he inevitably made contact. I loved everything about Ichiro Suzuki.

He figures prominently in many of my baseball memories, but none moreso than the single greatest afternoon I have ever spent at a ballpark, at the Rogers Centre in Toronto on September 23, 2010. It was a getaway day, midday start on a Thursday. No crowd to speak of, but our section was studded with loud fans holding hand-painted Japanese signs. The M's were 26 games back in the AL West and the Jays were 14.5 games behind in the East. The game meant nothing. But it was Ichiro's lone trip to Toronto that season so I took my daughter, who was four, which is to say she was in her fifth year of having my love of Ichiro forced upon her.

Ichiro was chasing a record that day. He was two hits shy of a tenth consecutive season with 200 or more hits, which no one had ever done (Pete Rose had ten non-consecutive years with 200-plus). I wore my Seattle 51 jersey for the occasion, which is probably why a Japanese TV host spotted us on our way into the stadium and asked to interview me. A camera was pointed at my face, a man with an enormous pompadour shouted at me in Japanese and pointed a mic at me, and a woman stood behind him holding a clipboard, translating his questions into English: "Where are you from?" "Why do you love Ichiro?" "Do you come to every game?" "What would the record mean to you?" I answered as best I could but it was a bewildering experience. I have no idea who, if anyone, ever saw that video. I don't imagine it made for very good TV.

We sat in the right field stands so we could better watch him play his position. He struck out to lead off the game but then smacked a double in his second at-bat and stood one hit shy of the record. In his next trip up he hit a sharp single to centre and stood at first base, the holder of another record. We rose to our feet, my daughter and me, along with 12,500 or so others, and applauded. My daughter screamed. I whooped. The Jumbotron flashed a graphic commemorating the achievement and then slowly dissolved into a shot of Ichiro standing at first, his face steely and blank. There's a game to be played, his focused eyes said. We took his cue and the game resumed.

Had that been all, it would have been a memorable day at the ballpark. But atop Ichiro's record that afternoon José Bautista hit his 50th home run of the season, the first Blue Jay to reach that plateau, and Félix Hernández tossed a two-hit complete game, taking the loss despite pitching masterfully (it was an effective thumbnail sketch of his season, in which he went 13–12 but still won the AL Cy Young). In the late innings, former Expo and then-Mariner bullpen coach John Wetteland tossed my daughter a ball, which she caught at the railing out in right field. She met the Jays mascot and after the game we wound our way down ramps, walked through the visitors' dugout, and stepped out onto the field, where she ran the bases with several dozen other children. When we left the stadium the Japanese TV crew interviewed me again on the steps outside. We went home happy.

In the days since I have inventoried my experience to come up with a more amazing afternoon, something featuring the same combination of family and fandom, access and history, and save for the really big ones (wedding, childbirth, etc.) I have come up short. There are no more perfect ballpark days than that one, spent with my little girl and my favourite player. The final score was 1–0 Jays but that number fails to capture the joy I can still unpack from the memory of that afternoon.

The years have piled up but Ichiro has continued to offer a pleasing opacity. He's been a quiet and stoically unreadable fixture in constant warming motion, his unending stretching, bending, lunging, and flexing providing a silent castigation of unpreparedness and sloth. For me, the most remarkable aspect of his career since has not been *what* he has done—for he has continued to do what he has long done—but where he's done it. In the midst of the 2012 season he was traded from the Mariners (my second-favourite team) to the Yankees (my least-favourite team), and I had to find a way to cheer for him despite the pinstripes adorning his jockey's frame. It was a challenge, but not an insurmountable one; I managed to pull for him while maintaining my chilly feelings for his employer.

These are the strange rules we draw for ourselves as fans, the stabilities we cling to in an inconstant world. He became the subject of yet another clause in the impossibly labyrinthine treaties of my own fandom. The agreements, détentes, and motivations that determine who we cheer for in a given game are as convoluted as those that plunged Europe into the First World War, and are similarly based not on logic but on sentiment, grudges, history, and chance. As far as I was concerned, the ideal outcome for his New York tenure would have been for the Yanks to be one-hit 162 times, the lone hit being an inside-the-park homer for Ichiro.

But heroes, toward the end, tend to wander. It's not so uncommon though it still seems strange. It looks like the Babe in a Boston Braves uniform. It looks like Frank Thomas in a Blue Jays cap. It looks like Ichiro at a press conference in Tokyo slipping on a crisp white Marlins home jersey with black, orange, yellow, and electric blue highlights, taking his coiled-spring grace and his slap-and-scamper routine to Miami after two-and-a-half seasons in the Bronx. The move was off-script, maybe, but not unforgivable. As the universe tends toward entropy, so too do joints, muscles, slash lines, careers. Sluggers' late career paths are largely predetermined; provided they can still slug, there's a place for them somewhere as designated hitters or maybe slow-footed first basemen. It was harder to know what the twilight would hold for Ichiro, though, who was never a slugger but something altogether different. He was 41 when he joined the Marlins, an age of declining speed, slowing reflexes and a short hop to total irrelevance—but we couldn't guess what Ichiro would do at 41 and beyond because we'd never seen a player quite like Ichiro.

It shouldn't have surprised anyone that to Miami he brought his inveterate dedication and the gravity with which he had always approached the game—a seeming scientific-spiritual amalgam. The Marlins' vaunted young outfield—Giancarlo Stanton, Christian Yelich, and Marcell Ozuna—ran into injury trouble that summer and so Ichiro played in 153 games in his first year in South Florida, adding 91 hits to his career total. When he signed on for another year with Miami after the 2015 season, it suggested he'd have the chance to add still more.

He retains a feline agility even as the grey continues to creep up his dome and down toward his chin. His numbers have dropped a tick, and maybe, just maybe, more balls fall around him than was once the case. But heading into the 2016 season he needs just 65 hits to reach 3,000—in America. Were you to add the 1,278 he collected with the Orix BlueWave of Nippon Professional Baseball (NPB), he's already hit safely 4,213 times, which puts him ahead of Cobb and only 43 hits behind Pete Rose's "unreachable" record.

This is astonishing, but then Ichiro's made a habit of threatening or besting gaudy records. Nobody was ever going to beat George Sisler's single-season hits record of 257. Then Ichiro chased down and finally overcame it in the summer of 2004.

It's true that he's not the same player he was then. That's unavoidable, and it raises the fear in some of us—and who knows, maybe in the man himself—that he'll show up to the park one day and, like so many before him, find that his skills have slipped below a respectable level and a swift exit will be the only dignified recourse left to him. Then, one day not too long thereafter, Ichiro—prolific hitter, scholar of baserunning, and the best right fielder a good many of us have ever seen—will go into the Hall of Fame, likely on the first ballot, and almost certainly wearing a Mariners cap, his legend undiminished by his denouement.

But what seems a shade more likely, and far more just, is that there'll be concentrated bursts of Ichiroian brilliance, a sporadic continuation of his absurd and idiosyncratic mastery of the game. This was the trend in the Bronx and will be the case in Miami. Not a lessened Ichiro, but simply less of him, until finally, one day, the hero is gone.

THE GRANDSTAND

It's at the far end of a leafy city park. You'll see the light stanchions first, among the trees, which comes as a relief because your directions just kind of left you back there at the corner with nothing to indicate where the baseball game would be played.

Closer, you see a covered grandstand, the kind of thing that would never be built today because no reasonable city council could or would justify the expense of that roof. But you'll be grateful it's there. It's stood for decades, welcoming people like you and shielding them from the hard sun and the drenching rain. Park behind it if you can. That's a good spot.

And then you move through the chain-link fence's gate and around the side where you pay the women at the folding table for an already torn ticket. Face the grandstand, then mount the stairs to the back rows. That's where you'll sit and it's as good a place as any.

There are a dozen or so rows of bleacher seating, rickety wooden benches painted grey. They hit you square in the lumbar region. At the very top of the bleachers there is a booth, and inside it sits a man with a microphone and a roster sheet. Below him maybe a few dozen souls are scattered across the seats: families, friends, parents, and perhaps grandparents of the players on the field. And there's also you, with the perfect feeling of being among them: these glad-hearted citizens, children, stout old men hunched on worn-out seat cushions wearing flat caps and ortho shoes. This is semi-pro baseball on a Tuesday night in a town you don't know, and everyone is there for their own obscure reasons.

You're here for baseball—because baseball is love and you'd follow it anywhere—but also just to be in some new place, somewhere removed from life as you so precisely know it. You drove west and south and you kept going until you found the place. The idea was to get a bit lost, turned around, to temporarily take leave of your bearings.

And it's working, as a shiver runs up the length of your body, starts in your toes and traces a line beneath your skin all the way to your scalp. The night's getting cool. Put on a sweater and wrap a blanket around your legs; done up like that you're so happy that you don't know what to do with your arms. You flail a bit, wrap them around yourself, throw them over the back of the bench, fold them on your knees. It's important to remember that it doesn't matter what you do with your arms.

What you really want to do is cast your arms wide and embrace the game in front of you. The field and the lights, rich soft grass, players in their uniforms made up of elements borrowed without permission from major league teams. Pop songs play on the tinny, overmatched conical loudspeaker dangling from the roof of the grandstand. All of that: hug it. You want to gather it all in your arms and claim it and never let anyone spoil it. You want to protect it as it has protected you. This is a reasonable thing to want, but also it's impossible.

So sit back and pull the blanket a bit tighter. You watch a big looping curveball from a lefthander whose name you will never know and then you look at the sky, which has gone from a pillowy soft gray to purple and then to blue-black, like a silent secondary show beyond the game. Night has come down—a soft summer night, and you, and all of the scattered fans and family members, are under the spell of some languid contentment that feels both pleasingly timeless and tragically ephemeral. Here now, blessedly, but also not for long.

That chill in the air suggests something you're not ready for, so you ward it off and cry out to the visiting team's batter, who is arguing a called strike even though his team is up a literal dozen runs.

Love this tiny grandstand, these people, the teams of unpolished players, a game that means nothing. Maybe you've always had a minor league heart? Mull this over while down at the snack bar, where the popcorn is bagged and the cans of Coke are doled out a dollar a pop. The 50/50 number is drawn and members of a local dance team encourage you to rise up for the seventh-inning stretch. You're not having any of that, though. You finally got the blanket just right.

News of the night's big league games drift in on your phone like rumours from a lost continent. Stuff it back into your pocket and forget about it; the highlights will be easy to find later. Better, clearly, to turn your attention back to these nameless men and the devotion it takes for the visitors to ride a bus on a Tuesday night, play a game, then climb back aboard for the ride home.

Or the love that drives members of the home team to do all this and then, say, sling an equipment bag over their backs, climb onto their bicycles, and head out into the dark streets, bound for houses and apartments where partners or roommates wait to say nothing more than "How was the game?" You want to remind yourself that it exists—love and devotion to a vast and difficult thing that might return little or nothing at all.

An unshakable truth resides in the score up there, the balls and strikes and outs. Everything accounted for, everything plain.

Lean in, then. Might as well. Elbows on knees, feet propped on the seat in front of you to better hear it, smell it, see it. You want to be deep within it, to lay down in the grass and feel the game moving around you. You want a shortstop to leap over you. You want a well-struck ball to zip sizzling over your head. Failing that, be happy to sit here, to take deep breaths, to fuss with your cap. To watch a sharp liner hit out to right, to hear the crack of it and to be reminded of what brought you here, down highways and back roads and streets you've never seen: the love, the small offer of devotion you know is represented by such a trip.

This is a devotion likely never recognized, but real and full all the same, and uniquely rewarding for the devotee. To see the scar of light against the inky sky, to let the sight of players fielding and throwing, swinging and running, work on your muscles like a proxy, both instructive and imitative, a nearly unreal echo of exertion that mirrors your own desire to live in your body.

Mostly you want to know this is real, that people gather to play ball all over the place, in towns and parks like this, here and everywhere. That others gather to watch. That they have done so for better than a hundred years and will continue to do so long after you are dead and gone. You want to step into a softly moving current that extends well beyond your life, and in so doing to forget your life and its many particulars, if only for nine innings. You want to forget where you came from, where you woke up, where you'll have to return once the game is over.

The long drive ahead can't be avoided, of course. The road lies expectant. The lock awaits your key. Once the game has ended, the home team defeated and all the good people drift home, once the visitors' bus has rolled out and the stanchions have been extinguished, you'll go. That is the thing to do.

But also: a last look at the grandstand, now dark. Then it's time to get your bearings on these alien streets and find the highway out of town. But take the pleasure to be found there, too, in the endless unfurling, the songs on the radio, a faraway voice recounting the day's scores.

Take comfort in where you've been and what you've seen. Bear up in the knowledge that it will all happen again tomorrow, in other towns you'll never know, in innumerable other places to get lost. Scan the dial for a game. Drive and think about baseball. Be grateful for it. Get yourself home, and as you slip into bed recognize you've placed your faith and love in something that will outlive you. Be glad you went.

THE D-TRAIN AT REST

Odds are you first saw Dontrelle Willis in 2003 and what you noticed was his leg kick, which was impossibly high and violent to the point where Willis nearly kneed himself in the jaw with each pitch he delivered. It was the first movement of a sequence that looked mostly wrong, but also childishly right—it was a motion you might have concocted as a kid, as seemingly logical as spinning your arm a dozen times before launching the ball. Willis went into a full-body twist, head rolling back, shoulders rotating, his back fully visible to the hitter, as though he was asking opposing batters, "Do you know my name yet? Here it is."

And then the lunge, a massive torquing stress on his body as he fell toward home plate, a lashing forward so erratic-seeming that it suggested Willis didn't quite know where home was and that there was no guarantee his pitch would find it. Finally the long-limbed release, his left arm unspooled like a cast line, followed by a sudden, jarring recoil. All this, over and over: batters retired, innings ended, Willis taking long strides off the field.

He was a sensation. This being 2003, they called him D-Train, first in South Florida and then beyond. His 14 wins nudged the Marlins into the playoffs that year, a 21-year-old ace suddenly playing for national TV audiences. In Game 4 of the NLDS he went 3-for-3 at the plate—he could hit, too—and the Fish eliminated the Giants.

Then ancient Jack McKeon (has there ever been a manager more appropriate to a team's local demographics?) and the Marlins, with an assist from Steve Bartman, broke the Cubs' hearts, rolled into the Series, and took the Yankees in six. When all was said and done, Willis was Rookie of the Year and a World Series Champion. And all of it with a smile on his face, all of it at 21, not nearly so long ago as it seems now with Willis's career at an end after a last attempt at a comeback—one of many after his magic deserted him—in which he was unable even to make it to the mound for the Milwaukee Brewers in the spring of 2015.

If you needed one word to sum Willis up you could do worse than exuberant. He had an energy that seemed to pour from every part of him at once. His face, his fingertips, down to his cleats. He radiated something good.

Which is not to say that it would have been nice to stand in against that motion of his. Imagine the ball exploding from that tangle of limb and leather—fastball running up to 96 mph and a changeup that looks just like the heater until it doesn't. The pitch hammers in or drops suddenly or creeps by, and then Willis is bounding off the field and grinning in a way that makes it damn near impossible to hold any malice.

His performance dipped in 2004 but it looked like he could find it again. It probably only required some infinitesimal adjustment to that seemingly improvised delivery of his. And there it was: Willis rebounded in '05, his finest year and a bit of hot magic. Everything clicked: the limbs, the lunge, the release. He won 22 games, struck out 170, finished second in National League Cy Young voting. The overall vibe was exceedingly positive, though distant early warning signs were there: in 2006 he hit 19 batters in 34 starts, a career high. That's the thing about exuberant deliveries: when they're off, they're *off.*

After a couple more seasons, none as electric as that one, Willis was packaged with Miguel Cabrera and shipped to Detroit for a haul, and the Tigers signed him for three expensive years.

There are those whose misfortune gives us some quiet pleasure or affirms some idle and uncharitable judgment of their character. Not so with Dontrelle, who was a mess in Detroit, the victim of injuries and what appeared to be the sudden and sinister disappearance of whatever alchemy he'd harnessed in Miami. Even when it was clear he didn't have what had once made him so dominant he still inspired a kind of good-natured boosterism in fans, residue of the wonder first inspired by that smile, that mesmerizing delivery, the blazing memory of what he too-briefly was— whatever the reason, no one who cared about baseball did not care about Dontrelle or want him to regain his form.

In June 2010 the Tigers traded him to Arizona for Billy Buckner (Twitter handle: @NotThatBB). Willis was jobless by July. Then came the bouncing-around years—Giants-Reds-Phillies-Orioles-Cubs—before he found himself in independent ball in '13. A couple of stints in the affiliated minors and then his last deal, with the Brewers, by which point even optimists had quit counting Dontrelle Willis's comeback attempts. It was only ever an outside shot. He hadn't pitched in a major league game in over three years. But it was a shot.

In the end, though, his body wouldn't give him any more. "The physical part of it," Milwaukee manager Ron Roenicke said after Willis's retirement was announced, "has worn on him." The body is with us and then it is against us.

Sometimes phenoms fizzle. Dontrelle Willis fizzled, in a way, but refused to be extinguished. He kept lifting that right leg and twisting and lunging in a teetering, off-kilter leap from the rubber toward the plate. He kept smiling, the cap crooked atop his head. He gave interviews and laughed and played along. *Don't let it break your heart*, the smile said, *I'm playing a game.* The motion—leg, twist, lunge, release—said, *Hey, you have control and then you lose it. But at least you had it.* As what he had deserted him, he never changed his approach or pitched like anyone else. Willis leapt at the challenge even in defeat.

Of all the might-have-beens and once-weres I can recall, none continued to churn so enthusiastically even after it was obvious his best days lay behind him. He was a bit goofy, D-Train, as endearingly askew as baseball's spin-centric modern age would allow. He had two great seasons, some middling ones, and some bad ones. He was out there, he had his moment, and he did it all with a smile on his face. That is what we will remember, and we will remember it.

THE GREEN LIGHT

John Gibbons sits on his hands because his baserunner knows. The baserunner is trusted. The baserunner is free to make his own decision.

Rajai Davis of the Blue Jays takes his lead off first, manager John Gibbons mute in the dugout, his team locked in a scoreless tie with Colorado, bottom of the eighth. Davis opened the inning with a single to right and now he stands on base, waiting.

A hitch in the pitcher's delivery, a gap, a window. There comes a point in the game, in the count, when everyone—every player, every coach, everyone in the stands—knows the baserunner is going. His right foot is on the turf, feet spread wide, he's bent low and his right hand swings like a pendulum. His fingers twitch. He's going. He's just waiting on that window. The pitcher knows. He needs to throw a strike, to deliver smoothly and quickly, to get the ball to a spot where the catcher can do something with it.

The catcher knows. He can feel it already, the motion of catching the ball even as he rises and begins cocking the ball back. He can already feel it in his shoulder, his elbow, his fingers. His job in the next moment is clear and simple: get the ball to second base before the baserunner.

But with the right jump from first it won't matter what the catcher does. That's the fact of it. A fast-enough player—the sort who has earned a perpetual green light—need only get a good jump, the proper start, and he has second base in his pocket. Head down, arms pumping, legs churning, a furious three seconds culminating in an explosion of dirt and a call of "Safe!" Rickey Henderson stole a base 130 times in 1982, and 1,406 times over the span of his career. You can bet Henderson had a green light. Number two on the all-time list is Lou Brock with 468 fewer swipes; he stole 118 in 1974. Brock had a green light too.

On the base paths, as elsewhere on the diamond, the manager is master. The green light is assent, permission. It's a blank cheque, the memo of which reads: I trust you. It's up to you.

Green lights are a potent symbol, of course, within baseball and without. They denote motion, speed, permission. The green light is promise and hope and the bestowal of trust. The term is so pervasive it has slid into usage as a verb: to green light. To grant approval. To agree to move forward. To give consent, thereby betting the fate of an enterprise on the success of a single endeavour.

The green light, in Fitzgerald's hands, is also the thing just over the horizon, the dormant promise, the improbable desire. The prize.

The Blue Jays need Rajai Davis in scoring position. They need him to reach second base. How he does so is up to him, because by virtue of his speed and instinct he's earned the green light from Gibbons. No coach relays Gibbons' wishes to Davis via signals. Davis doesn't need to glance into the dugout looking for the gesture that suggests he ought to go, here, on this pitch. Now. No, now.

Rajai Davis, successful on 12 of 13 stolen base attempts to this point in the season, and swiper of 235 sacks in his career, knows he's free to go when the opportunity presents itself. And he knows his team needs him in scoring position, now, or anyway very soon.

With the count 2–0 to Colby Rasmus, Rockies righty Matt Belisle throws a fastball. Davis explodes. It's both thrilling and disheartening to watch a body go so suddenly from rest to motion, displaying a readiness, a hair-trigger connection between brain and muscle, that the vast majority of us will never know. Davis is still and then he's a blur. Its violence is jarring. He has transformed from nonchalance to fury in a sliver of a heartbeat.

Three seconds, give or take. The world is hung up there, completely. Nothing else exists. It's marvellous, I'll think later, to forget everything and care only about this one outcome. Wilin Rosario, the catcher they call Baby Bull, rises and throws so suddenly that his mask slips from his head. The ball is airborne, on a line between his hand and second base, while Davis chugs along the baseline toward second, that point of convergence where he will meet the base and the ball will find a glove and the glove will swipe down to brush Davis's arm or leg or shoulder, and an umpire will adjudicate on the matter of which happened first.

There he goes, the announcer says. We all say. Sitting at home, it's what I say. When I'm in the stands, it's what I say, to myself and anyone nearby, in a low voice that seems appropriate to a moment of such bald reckoning. There he goes, meaning: Here we go. Meaning: Something is about to be decided, and all we can do is watch.

DEFUNCT

I'm waiting on a package. It's somewhere between here and Seattle, and it contains a trove of loss and defeat: three ball caps from minor league baseball teams that no longer exist. This is a thing I do. It's one of my favourite things, actually.

Relocated, renamed, contracted, defunct. The history of professional sports is littered with teams that failed, moved, or slipped quietly away. And I love them. The St. Louis Browns (American League, 1902–1953). The Indianapolis Hoosiers (Federal League, 1914). The Hamilton Red Wings (PONY League, 1939–1956). The package making its slow, meandering way toward me contains the bright red cap of the Habana Leones who last played in the Cuban League in 1961, the black cap and orange O of the Ottawa Giants who existed only for the 1951 International League baseball season, and the kelly green cap with a gold H of the Hawaii Islanders who made a go of it in the Pacific Coast League from 1961–1987. These teams—the knowledge of them, the evidence they left behind, and replica merchandise featuring their logos—fascinate and excite me. The obvious question is why?

Authenticity is a thing we may move toward but never touch; if it's to be found at all, it approaches us. But make no mistake, in buying these caps and memorizing the names of players and owners and stadiums from 20 years ago or better I'm attempting to will myself toward something authentic.

Two lost teams conspired to stoke my interest as a kid: the Brooklyn Dodgers and the Seattle Pilots. The Dodgers you know—they moved to LA and everything was swell except the borough of Brooklyn never forgave Walter O'Malley and didn't get a pro sports team again until the NBA's Nets forsook New Jersey in 2012. The Dodgers' Brooklyn years exist now as a fondly regarded ancestral history for a team that is unmistakably Californian. The Pilots are a bit more obscure. Seattle, longtime home of the minor league Rainiers (Pacific Coast League, 1919–1968), was awarded an American League expansion team for the '69 season. The Pilots, as they were named, played in the Rainiers' old park, a supposedly temporary measure until a larger domed stadium could be built. But the team quickly slid into bankruptcy and a Milwaukee used car salesman named Selig snapped them up. By Opening Day 1970 they'd moved to a different state and been rechristened the Brewers. Twenty years later I stumbled on this lurid bit of history in a book of baseball trivia, on the last page of which was a photo of a skeleton wearing a Pilots hat with the caption: "Seattle Pilots, 1969–1969." That discovery created in me a great desire to know the names and fates of all lost baseball teams, a desire I have yet to satisfy, though Lord knows I have tried.

I've always been interested in history, so that plays a role, but this desire to know baseball's past isn't academic; it's a deep and furious nostalgia, albeit of a misplaced, borrowed, or adopted sort. The word nostalgia is concocted from the Greek *nostos*, meaning homecoming, and *algos*, for pain. The ache of going, or wanting to go, home. This condition of mine is a curious variant because nothing about my home or my past has anything remotely to do with Sick's Stadium in Seattle or Ebbets Field in Brooklyn. What we're dealing with here is the longing for a feeling we've glimpsed or known before, a pastoral contentment wrapped up in a sense of community, as well as that slippery notion of authenticity—the desire for something real and honest and unstaged, unsullied by irony or commerce.

This feeling, this misplaced nostalgia, is a thing we're collectively suffering a terrific bout of—not just a desire to know about the past but to actually live it. In the midst of this postmodern malaise we don't just want to watch *Mad Men* and appreciate its fidelity to the time period in which it's set; we want to drink old fashioneds and dress like Don Draper. It's pandemic, really, and aspects of this widespread feeling are easily linked to contemporary urbanism, with its love of antiquated things, ironic display, and unprofitable small-scale industry (craft beer, moustache wax, suspenders, fixed-gear bicycles, etc.). It's a response, you might argue, to the uncertainty of our times, the perceived soullessness and homogeneity of modern life. Whatever the cause, I'm particularly prone.

So my backward-looking form of self-expression is to drape myself in the uniforms of dead baseball teams, and though I'd like to claim otherwise it is doubtless tinged by the snobbishness widely associated with pointedly arcane pursuits. I like knowing this stuff in large part because a lot of people don't know about it. It's another way to define and differentiate myself ("Oh, you like baseball? Yeah, your hat is cool, but ever heard of the Cienfuegos Elefantes?"). Mostly, though, it's an innocent love taken to an extreme. Those early discoveries of the Dodgers and Pilots, combined with my own experience of loss—the Montreal Expos, the Ottawa Lynx (International League, 1993–2007)—sent me running into the loving arms of Ebbets Field Flannels, makers of those caps I'm awaiting. The folks at Ebbets— and forgive me if this sounds like an ad but I'm boundlessly enthusiastic about their products — lovingly design and make gorgeous, high-quality reproductions of caps, jerseys, and jackets of long-gone teams in the minor and Negro leagues. Their continued success points to the existence of plenty of people similarly afflicted with my particular strain of nostalgia. Ditto Philadelphia's Mitchell & Ness, a "Nostalgia Co." that has thrived since they transitioned from supplying actual uniforms to recreating the logos and uniforms of yesteryear. Even the big guys have gotten in on the action with the explosion of major league teams wearing throwback uniforms on the field.

It isn't possible, of course, to actually root for a team that no longer exists. But the celebration of dead teams seems to me nevertheless consistent with the celebration of sport in general. Sports lend themselves to nostalgia because of the oral tradition, their long histories, and the way we measure players' performances against those who played decades ago. My grandmother used to tell me about her days of playing basketball on her high school team in the 1920s, and my father regaled me with tales of buying standing room only tickets at Maple Leaf Gardens.

The heart aches sweetly for things long lost and never to return. The caps, jerseys, and T-shirts are the ghostly evidence of things that existed: ballparks and the players who played in them, and the people who watched, who revelled communally in victory and suffered together in defeat. They're elements of a past for which I long, pointlessly. The past is perfect because we can never go back there. It's a safe precinct in which any disappointments have already been suffered and none will take us by surprise. The Pilots will always move to Milwaukee, the Islanders will always leave Hawaii, and the Dodgers are always bound for the West Coast. There is comfort to be found in the act of remembrance, in the notion of memory's long reach, for if some still take the time to learn of the history of the Montreal Royals (Eastern League, 1897–1911; International League, 1912–1918, 1928–1960), or the New York Cubans (Negro National League, 1935–1936, 1939–1950), perhaps in a hundred years the world will still know something of us.

MARCO SCUTARO HITS
A FOUL BALL

It's sometime between '97 and '03, though I'm betting on the earlier end of that. Let's say it's '99—that would square with my own personal chronology, given that during the events chronicled here I'm sitting in the cold, concrete, largely empty V of Ottawa Stadium next to the woman who will later become my wife—and Marco Scutaro is up to bat. In puzzling over the date on baseball-reference. com and cross-checking it with thebaseballcube.com, I'm amazed that Scutaro—who won the 2012 NLCS MVP by batting .500 despite being bowled over so forcibly by a Matt Holliday slide into second base that he was taken for X-rays to ensure his hip wasn't broken—played in Triple-A for parts of seven seasons, all of them in the International League. Do you think he was sick of that circuit? Were there times he said to himself, *Jesus, not another goddamn game in Scranton, or Richmond, or, oh lord, Ottawa?* Do you think there were more than a few nights in shitty motels when Marco Scutaro was just about ready to give the hell up?

So yeah, let's say it's 1999, early in the season, probably April, May at the latest, a night game between the Buffalo Bisons and the Ottawa Lynx. Cold, damp, and dreadful. The stands of the ballpark in Ottawa, which haven't been regularly full since the '95 season when the Lynx beat the Norfolk Tides to win their only Governor's Cup, are all but empty. The concession stands have run out of coffee and hot chocolate so I've come back to my seat with another beer. The first sip from the plastic cup is sloshy and gassy. My hands are cold.

Scutaro's name is announced. I pronounce it "Scoo-TAHR-o," probably because the PA man says it that way, though by the time Scutaro makes his big league debut in '02 with the Mets the media guides will carry a guide to pronouncing it closer to the way he himself says it: "SCOOT-aro." I've seen him before when the Bisons have come to town but he hasn't been particularly memorable. "Italian?" asks my future wife. "Uh," I say, checking the lineup one-handedly, "Venezuelan."

I don't remember who's pitching for Ottawa so I'm free to make it up. Let's say it's Mike Johnson, who'll win 6 and lose 12 in '99 but earn a September cup of coffee with Montreal anyway based on his peripherals. In later years he'll spend some more time with the Expos, bounce around the minors, do a short stint in Japan and end up finishing his career in the independent leagues.

I do remember this: our seats are in the first row behind the Lynx dugout on the third base side. We sit with our feet up on the concrete roof of the dugout while below it the players spit and laugh and brood and try to figure a way out of Ottawa, the minors, baseball purgatory. A few will make it, most will not.

It's not quite right to say that I am also, at this same moment, looking for a way out of Ottawa, though I'm certainly amenable to the idea. It's a town not wholly devoid of charms but at the age of 22 they're largely lost on me. Or maybe it's that, having spent most of my life in the city, I just don't care to seek them out anymore. I've escaped the suburbs, exhausted the all-ages punk show scene, frequented the same bar for far too long, dropped out of Carleton University (though I'll be back there in a few years for a second kick at the can), completed a tour of the service industry, written precious little despite the fact that writing is my oft-stated goal, and watched a steady parade of friends move away. I know nothing. My goals are vague, my ambitions ill-defined. At this moment my certainties are few, but one of them is that the woman sitting beside me will save me from aimlessness and drift. You watch. She'll believe in me despite scant evidence to support her hunch. She'll convince me to buy a house in the country, marry me, bear our children. She'll carry me through. Tonight she humours me, sitting in a cold, nearly abandoned ballpark, watching a meaningless minor league game, her head and hands wrapped tight, her butt surely as frozen as mine. She keeps score with a dull pencil. She cheers when appropriate. It's simply another night spent away from our apartment; we could just as easily be in a pub or a restaurant or at a friend's place watching a movie. We are young and childless and we have time to fill.

Scutaro steps in. He's a righty so his back is to us. Johnson throws some pitches. I don't know what the count is. There's a man on base, or there isn't. It won't matter. Johnson goes into his delivery, rears back, takes his long stride...

In my life to this point I have caught one souvenir baseball. It happened a few years ago at this very ballpark when I sat down the first base side with a friend. Rochester was in town and their first baseman was Calvin Pickering, a big, lumbering slugger in the mold of Mo Vaughn or Cecil Fielder. I suppose Baltimore had hopes he'd learn to stay healthy and cut down on his strikeouts. He did neither. But on that night he hit a dribbling foul ball down the first base side and Rochester first base coach (and former Pirate, Phillie, Expo, and Padre) Dave Cash picked it up, turned around and lobbed it to me. After the game Pickering stood next to the vistors' dugout signing autographs. He signed my ball. That was a nice memory to be sure, but the nature of the acquisition—tossed lightly by a first base coach—made it feel as though the ball bore an asterisk. It wasn't a true foul ball caught, earned; it was happened upon.

But on this night I'm in a prime location to get a ball. I await my opportunity with raw hands, a cold beer in my grasp. Johnson is in his follow-through now, having just released a breaking ball from his fingertips and Scutaro is ahead of it but he recognizes this in time and slows his swing, just hoping to make contact. He flails at the ball with his bat way out in front of the plate, the bat head swinging sideways through space, coming across toward third instead of straight out to centre. The ball glances off the tip of the bat and it zips toward the Lynx dugout. En route it skips almost imperceptibly off the damp grass then kicks high.

I don't know when I stopped bringing a glove to baseball games. At some point, I suppose, I reckoned that the chances I'd need it were dwarfed by the odds it'd make doing things I was sure to do—read the lineup card, drink beer, eat popcorn, clap—a bit of a pain in the ass. Maybe it speaks to a loss of faith, the death of the belief that among thousands of people I'd be the one toward whom an earthbound ball would head. In that light it's a bit heartbreaking, isn't it, coming to terms with the unfeeling realities of our world? Or maybe I just figured out that at Ottawa Lynx games the easiest way to get a foul ball was to watch which empty section it landed in and saunter over there later to pick it up. All of this is to say that on this cold evening at the ballpark on Coventry Road I have no baseball glove. And the ball Scutaro just hit has bounced off the grass in a trajectory that will take it over the lip of the dugout and right toward the point in space currently occupied by my head.

But I'm cool. Half-full beer in my left hand, I lean forward onto the balls of my feet like an infielder. My future wife gives a little shriek when she sees where the ball is headed, leans away and shields her head with her arms. My vision takes on a sharp, precise focus, a tunnel of light surrounded by blur and darkness. I tense and prepare. I have a fraction of a second to figure out what to do here. I have dismissed the idea of a clean catch based on the speed at which the baseball is screaming toward me, and the fact, previously mentioned, that I no longer bring a glove to games. I don't have time to consider that everyone in the ballpark is looking at me, even if it's only a few hundred shivering souls.

I raise my right hand shoulder-high and position it to roughly where I think the ball will go. It turns out I'm pretty accurate though my eyes can't have actually relayed that info to my brain—there was no time. There's an instantaneous calculation at play, a vectoring, a weighing of experience and guesswork. The ball touches my hand (I feel only an impact, no sting), there's a dull, meaty thwack, and I push upward shot-put style. The ball, now considerably slowed, lofts straight upward, perhaps ten feet over my head. I continue to watch it. I'm now standing bolt upright and still have a beer in my left hand. It's still half full.

The next moment is a long one. I have time to consider two possible outcomes. The first involves catching the rebounded ball cleanly and bringing this brief scene to a satisfying conclusion. The second ends in abject failure, possibly embarrassment. I want very badly for the first to occur.

Meanwhile, having apexed, the uncaring ball drops back toward earth, right toward me. There's a gasp from the small crowd—or do I imagine that? Is it from me?—as it nears. I flatten my right hand, the same hand off which the ball has so recently ricocheted, offering my palm to heaven like a penitent.

It lands like a feather. Like a balloon. It nestles gently and soundlessly into my hand and I close my fingers over it and hold it there a beat, afraid I have imagined the moment, afraid the ball is made of glass, or smoke, or dream. But I squeeze it and come to trust that, yes, it is substantial, it is real, it is firm and beautiful. I bring it down to a smattering of applause and I hold the thing in front of me as I retake my seat. Then I glance at my left hand and the beer still there, and happily discover I haven't spilled a drop. A rare, warm elation fills me. I have, to my own mind, pulled off an elusive stunt. I am quietly thrilled.

I want to say now that Scutaro has watched the whole thing, the long moment since he tipped a breaking ball down the third base line, and that he witnessed my act of balance and quick wit, maybe even tipped his batting helmet in my direction or at the very least smiled. But when I look back he is resettled in the batter's box, his back to us, bat waggling over his head and eyes fixed on Johnson, awaiting the next pitch.

The ball in my lap, I am fairly beaming. The woman by my side throws her arm over my shoulders. "Nicely done," she says and asks to see the ball. I hand it to her and she inspects the thing, feels its smooth hide, the surface rubbed down to a dull off-white, a scuff mark on its flank where it hit the grass.

"How's your hand?" she asks.

I look at it. Red, raw, it suddenly begins to throb and to sting, a heat coming into it. I can feel my palm swelling ever so slightly, the skin tightening. I can already feel the dull ache it will endure tomorrow.

"It's great," I say.

PROSPECTS

The Yankees took Brien Taylor first overall in 1991. When scouts looked at Taylor, a hard-throwing lefty who'd spent four years mowing down batters in a North Carolina high school, they had visions of Dwight Gooden. The fact that he was a southpaw only sweetened the deal. The Yanks offered Taylor $300,000 and looked forward to having him on the mound in the Bronx in just a few years' time. But then super-agent Scott Boras stepped in to "advise" Taylor and his family, and on the agent's recommendation the young pitcher held out for Todd Van Poppel money. The Yankees relented and ponied up $1.5 million. Taylor signed and headed to the Florida State League to begin his pro career.

Sometime in the summer of 1992 my parents and I drove south to visit friends in Virginia. My father was a naval officer and Bruce Johnston, one of his Navy buddies, had been posted to Norfolk. We stayed with him and his family and planned to see the sights, like Colonial Williamsburg, maybe make a sandcastle at Virginia Beach and dip our toes in the Atlantic.

The Johnstons had two boys, both older than me, but I knew them well. Navy families tend to latch onto one another as they do the Victoria-Ottawa-Halifax posting circuit (my father's naval postings had a big hand in determining the geographic circumstances of my family history; he and my mother met in Halifax, married in

Victoria, had my brother and sister in Halifax, and me in Ottawa). Christopher was older than me by a several years and was to my mind an adult, but his brother Keith was only a year or so older than me. We'd played together as younger boys and still had interests in common; we liked cars, enjoyed the same movies.

On this visit, after we'd cruised Virginia Beach, hit the mall, played minigolf, and watched a hundred hours of TV, we were kind of at ours wits' end. Chris and Keith, tasked with entertaining me while our fathers played golf and our mothers caught up, played their last hand: a Tidewater Tides game.

I'd been wearing my Blue Jays jersey around just about daily. It was a staple of my wardrobe. This was, after all, 1992, and in a few short months the Marine Color Guard would march onto the field at Atlanta-Fulton County Stadium and present an upside-down maple leaf. Otis Nixon would try to bunt and Mike Timlin would field it cleanly and flip it to Joe Carter at first and the Jays would mob one another in celebration of their first of World Series title. Afterwards, I and several friends would walk the streets of our suburban Ottawa subdivision shouting and using noisemakers while passing cars honked at us in solidarity. This is all intended to say that I was then, as I am now, baseball mad.

It was a thick, sweltering evening when Chris, Keith, and I rolled into the parking lot of decrepit Metropolitan Memorial Park in Tidewater, home of the New York Mets' top minor league affiliate. I hadn't yet read William Styron so I didn't have a literary grounding for the experience of Virginia heat. I was 16 years old, very much still a boy, and everything looked and felt new to me. The parking lot was nearly empty, a vast expanse of asphalt and light stanchions. As we walked the blacktop felt spongy beneath my feet.

We bought tickets—they were smallish tickets from a roll, the sort of thing I associated with raffles and fairs but not ball games—and ventured inside. The ballpark was a simple concrete grandstand with a poorly lit and musty concourse below. We were handed miniature binders with the Tides' logo on them and plastic card sleeves inside. This was the height of the card-collecting craze when every boy was certain he was building his fortune by amassing a stash of prime Upper Deck and Fleer and Topps selections, keeping them in mint condition in binders or hard plastic sleeves. We understood little of economic theory though and couldn't grasp that the long lineups of likeminded boys and men at card shows meant everybody would have the same Frank Thomas rookie card and it would therefore not pay for our early retirement. It was a lottery, was our thinking, and all those other suckers just weren't playing it right.

After we got popcorn and drinks and found our seats on the third base line beneath the cantilevered roof I opened the small binder to flip through its plasticky-smelling pages, and saw that the people who'd paid for the promotion (the Upper Deck card company, I believe) had seeded the thing with a single card: Brien Taylor. "Yankees Top Prospect," it read, and in the photo Taylor posed, right leg cocked, staring over his right shoulder toward an imaginary batter. He was in pinstripes. Over his head the bright blue sky of what I assume is Florida was dotted with puff white clouds as if to say the sky was the limit for an enormous talent like Taylor.

During the early innings I ducked back into the depths of the stadium where I bought a Tides cap and a white T-shirt with the Tides script on the front and the Mets logo on the back. The cap was what we'd now call a trucker hat, though then it was simply a hat. A minor league team didn't often offer fitted or official caps; the area of sports merchandising was decidedly less sophisticated in 1992. In time, the T-shirt faded and yellowed and the poly-cotton fabric became thin as paper. It's in a landfill somewhere now but the cap is still in my possession.

The cap was a bad fit, though I spent many minutes adjusting and re-adjusting the plastic strap, and once I had it on as comfortably as I could manage I went back to the seats. There was an older man sitting near us. Looked to be a season-ticket guy. He fit the profile: an unimpressed, leathery face, a worn seat cushion beneath his Hagar-clad rump, an ancient Mets cap atop his head. He bestowed the sense that the section in which we were seated was his living room, and indeed it may as well have been given the amount of time he probably spent there.

"What's in the book," he growled at me, pointing a bony digit imprecisely toward the card binder.

"Baseball cards," I said.

"Let's see," he commanded. I handed him the small, vinyl-wrapped book. He studied the cover then opened it up and looked through his bifocals at the Brien Taylor card.

"That kid's quite something, isn't he?"

"Yeah," I said, but the Johnston boys returned blank expressions. They had never heard of Taylor because they were not big baseball fans, though they were happy enough to be there in a nearly empty ballpark on a warm summer night in Virginia, sweaty Cokes in hand and nowhere else to be.

So season-ticket man and I filled them in on the accolades heaped on Taylor, his can't-miss designation and his great stuff, though neither of us had seen him throw a pitch. We pontificated and preached. I tried to match his wisdom, though of course I couldn't. But it was a wonderful way to pass an evening and I was grateful to him for talking to us. Sometime in the later innings someone hit a home run for the Tides (D.J. Dozier?) and it lofted high into the thick night air and over the right field fence. It drew our attention to the giant Marlboro Man sign—a dusty, leather-chapped cowboy carrying a saddle on his shoulder that rose high over the wall—and to the purpling sky with lightning flashing in the distance. By the time we drove home it had begun raining, a heavy, crashing downpour that lasted all night.

I don't remember if the Tides won. I don't even remember who they played, to be honest. In past years I'd have found the answer in my cigar box of ticket stubs, but that was taken when somebody broke into our house in the early '00s. They made off with a television, a camera, some cash, and the cigar box. It is, you will understand, the only thing taken that I miss.

In the days that remained of our trip to Virginia we went to the beach again and possibly to a movie, and Keith let me drive his cherry red 1977 Datsun 280 Z, which he'd bought off his high school librarian, on the freeway. I wore the Tides hat the whole time and probably looked foolish in it. Then my parents and I drove home.

In the years that followed Bruce Johnston was appointed Admiral and took up residence in a very fine house on CFB Esquimalt, Victoria. Christopher moved to Vancouver and Keith settled in Ontario. Our fathers are all retired now, the Navy and the life associated with it just a memory, though a fond one to hear them tell it.

Maybe you know some part of the end of this. The following season the Tides moved out of Metropolitan Memorial and into Harbor Park in downtown Norfolk. They took the city's name and left Tidewater far behind. The Met was torn down and picturesque Harbor set a new template of sorts for what the Triple-A leagues expected from their ballparks. Which is to say you'd never find a top affiliate playing in a park like the Met these days. All those stadiums have been replaced with newer, larger facilities, or the teams have relocated to communities eager to build them lavish new nests. Keith came to my wedding and charmed everyone there, telling jokes, folding his napkin into the shape of a chicken and making it dance. He later married his partner David, who runs a lovely restaurant near Manotick, south of Ottawa. They bought a nice house in the country, and some horses.

I got married and had three kids and now I write about baseball in my basement office filled with old scorecards, pennants, jerseys, and ball caps—including the Tides hat. The Brien Taylor card is probably down here somewhere too, though I don't know which box it's in. I've never thrown away a baseball card. Hope springs eternal.

Brien Taylor never pitched a major league inning for the Yankees or anyone else. In December 1993 he tore his labrum defending his brother in a fistfight. Surgery and rehab failed to make him the pitcher he had been at 19, and though he hung around the minors for a few different organizations he finally retired in 2000. He was only the second top overall pick to fail to reach the majors. As you'd expect for anyone who'd come so close to something so big, his life has been a bit uneven since. Drug charges, court dates, outstanding warrants, prison time, supervised release; these are not the stats anyone anticipated for Brien Taylor. But once upon a time his prospects were good.

ODDS AGAINST:
THE BALLAD OF RICKY ROMERO

It didn't have to go this way, but then maybe it did. This was, for Ricky Romero as for the vast majority of people who ever seriously endeavour to play a sport professionally, the statistically likely outcome: an inglorious end. In Romero's case, after a ten-year relationship with the lefthander the Toronto Blue Jays released him without so much as a press conference. A tenure with the team that began with Romero being selected sixth overall in the 2005 draft after leading Cal State Fullerton to a College World Series win ended with Romero injured and to all appearances broken for good by The Thing, an affliction that causes some pitchers to forget how to throw strikes.

All fanbases are tempted into games of What If: Draft Edition, but none with the relish of frustrated ones. In Blue Jays lore, the legacy of ex-GM J.P. Ricciardi can be summed up by the fact that Romero was taken one pick ahead of shortstop Troy Tulowitzki, and just a few before outfielder Andrew McCutchen. The Jays would get Tulowitzki eventually, trading away prospects, including another first-rounder, along with José Reyes, in the very same season that they released Romero. Tulowitzki's arrival helped spark the dramatic playoff push of 2015, and that success, along with the much higher salary the team ended up paying the shortstop than they would have had they drafted him, contribute to make the entirety of Romero's tenure with the Blue Jays appear as some kind of expensively corrected mistake.

The odds are always long. Of the first 100 picks in the 2005 draft, only 23 were on a big-league roster on the day Romero was cut. Romero was 30 years old, and from there on out nothing would get easier, but he at least made it to The Show before he was unmade. That's not nothing. But while Romero flashed promise—by Wins Above Replacement, Romero is still the third most valuable pitcher picked in that first round—he was never an MVP like McCutchen, nor a perennial All-Star like Tulo.

The unraveling was long and gradual and came very quickly to seem final. But when he was on Romero was something: a four-seamer that could touch 95 mph and a changeup that worked when the fastball was sharp, making hitters look off-balance and goofy. Twice during the Blue Jays' depressingly barren black-capped years he was the Opening Day starter, and in 2011 he was an All-Star. From 2009 through 2011 he won 13, 14, and 15 games, respectively, and remained mostly on the good side of the delicate control/wildness balance.

Then it all came unhinged, as mysteriously as these things ever do, during the second half of 2012. By Opening Day 2013 he was in A-ball; Romero made his last four major league appearances with the Blue Jays that year, getting 22 outs and allowing 20 baserunners, 11 of them by walk. He spent the next couple of years toiling away but never rising above Triple-A. There were surgeries, then recoveries, throwing sessions, and assessments. It was a bewilderingly Sisyphean process and rarely did the reports augur well. And then his release by the Blue Jays, as matter-of-fact and unsurprising as can be, but also a kind of hollow shock.

In announcing the move, Toronto GM Alex Anthopolous employed the bland and toothless corporate-speak that characterizes modern baseball communication: "We made the determination we just didn't think by the end of the year he was going to be able to factor for us up here. Knowing this was the last year of his contract, we felt it was best to just give him the opportunity to get a head start somewhere else." It was a business decision.

There is no solid moral purchase to find on the matter of how athletes are disposed of once they're no longer needed, but the hard fact is that there's nothing particularly notable about Romero's story. Athletes are paid to win, goes the argument. But also: this is an actual human who was paid to do a thing until it seemed like he wasn't very good at doing that thing anymore, at which point his employer said, publicly, "We can't use you anymore, but maybe somebody else can."

There did exist the chance that somebody else would find a way to fix Ricky Romero. Who knows? Those odds are glaringly pessimistic but comebacks have been made of far less likely stuff; Scott Kazmir was 27 when he lost the plate utterly and 29 when he found it again. But while the romantics among us hoped for a plot point in his redemption story, I held fondly the memory of Romero's big league debut.

The Jays hosted the Tigers that early April afternoon, and Romero matched up against fellow first-rounder and Great Hope for the Future Rick Porcello. It was the first time two first-rounders had made their debuts against one another. Romero outpitched Porcello that day, earning a 6–2 win on the strength of homers by Marco Scutaro, Aaron Hill, and Adam Lind. That was what the future looked like then for the Blue Jays and their fans. But that's the thing about futures: odds are they'll look different than you'd hoped.

KING FELIX'S CHANGEUP

Control is an illusion, or a partial one, anyway. It's best thought of as a degree of the whole rather than as something one can possess outright. Or maybe the pragmatic way to approach it is this: you control only so much, and everything else is out of your hands. The lesson to be learned from those whose success depends on control is that you should worry like hell over those things you can reasonably expect to influence, and not at all over the rest.

Félix Hernández's plow horse consistency stems from his understanding of the above. He's our case study. The 2,000th strikeout of his career came on a picture-perfect Sunday afternoon—Mother's Day 2015, as it happened—in the top of the fifth inning at Safeco Field. Oakland's Sam Fuld was the victim, caught looking at a fastball on the corner. At 29 years and 32 days, Hernández became the fourth-youngest pitcher to reach that milestone. Bert Blyleven, Walter Johnson, and Sam McDowell all did it a bit quicker, Nolan Ryan and Sandy Koufax just a tick slower. It bears noting that among that list all but McDowell are Hall of Famers.

When he collected his first strikeout at 19 by punching out Pudge Rodriguez, Hernández was all brawn, firing fastballs like unguided ordnance. But overthrowers don't have long careers, at least not until they learn, like Hernández has, that control is often the opposite of power.

Along the way he became a good deal more virtuosic, recognizing the nuance inherent in that distinction. Ten years on, two pitches before he notched Fuld as his 2,000th with a 92 mph heater, Hernández dropped in an 80 mph curve of giggle-inducing perfection. It was an exercise in control and it was, from any hitter's perspective, unfair.

But the ultimate proof of the knowledge he's gained lies in his perfection of the changeup, a pitch that requires one to feign power while operating with finesse. It's all guile and psychology. It requires mastery over one's own body— if it doesn't look exactly like you're cranking up a fastball then it isn't fooling anyone—and faith in its execution. It's what Félix Hernández can control—not declining velocity, not advancing age, not how many runs his team scores, not what happens during the four games between his starts—and the consensus is that in his hands it's one of the best pitches in baseball. His increasing reliance upon it constitutes something of a changeup too, as Félix's initial rise was the result of power, impulse, and abandon. He was a chucker, albeit an exceptional one, and if he had remained so hitters would have caught up with him. Instead he became a surgeon, his pulse registering barely a blip regardless of the situation. As Félix strode nonchalantly around the mound after K number 2,000 the ticket holders in The King's Court—the three-section swath of seats set aside for matching-shirted Félix fans during his starts at Safeco—were wild, unhinged. Meanwhile the man himself was all control, mature and restrained and in every sense a professional, even if draped in a uniform fully twice as big as necessary, a tattoo blaring brazenly off his neck.

Now about that neck tattoo. It's a stylized depiction of his astrological sign: Aries, the ram. Characteristics of those born under the sign of Aries, if you believe in such things, include independence, moodiness, and impulsiveness. Which is to say that getting an Aries-themed tattoo is a sort of self-affirming act, evidence mainly of itself. Hernández got it before the start of the 2013 season, shortly before signing an extension through 2019 with a team option for the year after that.

As he's aged that tattoo has come to look increasingly incongruous, a birthmark of impetuousness on someone progressively less impetuous and comfortable both with what he can control—the baseball, himself—as well as with what he can't.

Wins are something of an antique statistic, I grant you, but the fact is the Mariners stand a far greater chance of winning with Félix on the mound and tend to flounder when he isn't. His other numbers imply a cold precision; he gets cooler and more assured, but that tattoo remains, peeking above collars, obvious and unhidden. Maturity looks a little different for those who spend their early twenties making the best hitters in the world look foolish.

But it's also true that we are all Félix in a sense, if less wealthy and talented. We all carry with us a motley assortment of old decisions and the proof thereof; they are written on us, sometimes in places we can't conceal. We change too, and adapt, but we continue to live with what we've inscribed on ourselves and on the world. We are marked by youth but pulling ever away from it, watching it recede behind us. Félix Hernández did not remain the boy he was when he debuted; he got better. But the tattoo is ever appropriate. Some things can't be changed and shouldn't be concealed. Youthful enthusiasm, when it ages well, morphs into intractability and steadfastness. Félix Hernández was young until he wasn't, but what he does never changed, only how he does it.

How he differs from many of us is his apparent acceptance of all that. Many of us—I mean to obliquely implicate myself here—rail against the things we can't change. We dwell and bemoan and kick and regret. We practice extreme rites and rituals of self-castigation. Against all logic, we experience shame over failing to control uncontrollable things.

Félix Hernández's evolution and continued mastery is a study in the value of letting go of what's beyond your grasp. Control what little you can, it hints. King Félix doesn't play every day. He doesn't hit. It isn't his job to get runners over. The past is the past, the seasons roll on, bodies deteriorate, balls bounce funny, squeak by, fall in. None of that rests within his influence. He just pitches. Fastball, curve, slider, changeup. That's what he can control and the rest be damned.

TAGGED

My father once sat next to Kelly Gruber on an airplane. I don't remember where the plane was headed—my father used to travel a lot for business—but Dad took his seat and there, right next to him, sat the blond-haired third baseman. Well, ex-third baseman; this was sometime after his retirement. "Kelly Gruber!" Dad said. They shook hands.

I like to think that as a result of having grasped Gruber's paw, my father effectively tagged Deion Sanders on the foot too, completing the triple play that was a triple play in the eyes of everyone but the ump at second. I'll bet if you asked Sanders he'd tell you, if he were being honest, that he felt Gruber's glove brush his foot as he scampered back to the bag. Based on the unscientific study of his facial expression as he watched for the ump's call, I'm pretty sure Sanders knew he was out.

I'll back up in case the reference doesn't ring any bells. In Game 3 of the 1992 World Series, with no score and the Series tied at one, both Terry Pendleton and Deion Sanders reached base for Atlanta to start the fourth inning. Then David Justice hit a Juan Guzmán pitch deep to centre, which Devon White hauled in with a lovely catch against the SkyDome's blue plastic wall. Both Pendleton, the lead runner, and Sanders had taken off on the hit, assuming it would fall over White's head. When Pendleton and Sanders saw that White had caught the ball, they scrambled back toward their respective bases, and in the jumble Pendleton passed Sanders, thereby rendering himself out. White turned and fired a perfect pellet to Robbie Alomar, the cutoff man, who delivered the ball to John Olerud at first, unaware that Pendleton was already out. Olerud then threw across the diamond to Gruber at third. Sanders was trapped between bases. Shortstop Manny Lee was covering second but Gruber elected to run Sanders down, eventually lunging at Sanders as he dove back into the bag. Gruber swiped his glove, the ball therein, at Sanders' retreating foot.

Umpire Bob Davidson, right on top of the play, called Sanders safe. Gruber sprang up to argue the call, gesturing fervently at the base with the same hand my dad would shake a few years later. And the replay every Jays fan has seen a hundred times since confirms it: Gruber tagged Deion Sanders on the heel. By rights, the Blue Jays had executed just the second triple play in World Series history—the first out was Justice, coming on White's catch, Pendleton got himself out by passing the trailing runner as he retreated back to first and Sanders, number three, was tagged by Kelly Gruber's glove. But the third out was never officially recorded because Bob Davidson blew the call.

Blown calls define us. None among us has managed to escape the ignominy of being cheated, wrongly accused, or in some way misunderstood. These routine injustices are one of the ways in which the happy fate we know we deserve is waylaid or delayed, pushed further from us though agonizingly still in sight. By virtue of their frequency blown calls aren't special. What is noteworthy are the ways in which we accommodate or overcome these denied opportunities. If we meet failure, if we are denied success by the poor judgment of another and we allow it to mar our efforts thereafter, the blown call has beaten us. But if we emerge from such moments to convince the world of our merit then we restructure the narrative: the blown call has strengthened our resolve.

It's that first scenario I find interesting, though, because it's such a common human moment, when futility overtakes us and the world is deaf to our protest. You hear a comment that betrays someone's false impression of your actions. You sit dumb the moment you learn you've been denied advancement when you know, beyond ego and self-delusion, that you are the right candidate. That sensation of heat burns in your temples and at the top of your spine because you're right, damn it, you are right and they are wrong. You have been wrong before but in this you are right, unassailably so. This was your moment and through someone else's ineptitude or bias you're forced to watch the world play on in what seems to you an alternate reality, a living what-if scenario.

The play in question didn't win or lose the game. The third out came when Guzmán struck out DH Lonnie Smith, stranding Sanders at second. In the bottom of the inning Joe Carter hit a ball that cleared the fence in left. Atlanta rallied. Gruber hit one in the eighth to tie it at two and the Jays won in the bottom of the ninth when Candy Maldonado's sacrifice fly cashed in Alomar. After the game, when shown video evidence, Bob Davidson admitted he'd been wrong. Four nights later, on the infield grass of Atlanta-Fulton County Stadium, the Jays mobbed one another in celebration. The blown call didn't matter.

But what if it hadn't been so? What if the breaking ball that Guzmán threw to retire Smith had hung a bit, allowing the Braves' diminutive DH to pull it over the SkyDome fence, a two-run shot that put the Braves ahead for good? And what if that game proved the pivot, handing momentum to Atlanta, swinging the Series in their favour? Then what?

Gruber argued the call, as anyone would, because he knew what was at stake. He argued with a mixture of anguish and exasperation, neither one borne, I'm certain, of a desire to see his name affixed to such a rare feat but of a burning need to get out of the inning without giving up a run. Gruber wanted to win the game.

Why argue with an umpire, whose word is law? Because a lifetime in baseball teaches you to fight to the death for every run, every out. Gruber knew the importance of that out. So he argued.

Likewise, we argue because the stakes always feel dire even when they aren't. Innocence, virtue, credit; they are all too precious to cede without a fight. So we plead our case, each of us, whatever the scenario, with conviction and a sense of moral certitude. The injury of the blown call would otherwise be too much to bear.

All present in the still-new SkyDome that October night felt the sting of the injustice done to Gruber and the Blue Jays in the top of the fourth inning. There are plays you watch in person, with your hands hovering in space prepared to clap, and afterward you're not quite sure what you've seen. But everyone at the Dome, and everyone watching at home too, knew what they'd witnessed: Gruber, lunging, tearing his rotator cuff in the process, had tagged Sanders and completed a triple play, and Toronto had escaped the inning without surrendering a run. Only Bob Davidson didn't know.

The Blue Jays won the game, and the World Series, and the one after that, but in the moment Gruber couldn't know all that any more than he could know he'd be traded to the California Angels for Luis Sojo that off-season, and that an injury would see to it that he played his last game in '93. He was just trying to win a game. So he argued with a combination of frustration and anger, though he couldn't have actually believed the call would be changed.

And it's hard not to see yourself in that scenario: judged, unaware of what's to come, with no way of knowing that everything will turn out all right, and in that moment certain only of your own position. A call is blown and you know it, but it doesn't matter; the world, with all its rules and processes, has got you beat. For all your certainty, all your effort, it won't go down in the official record. You're left standing with the ball tucked in your glove and you're steaming.

"Come on," you're yelling, "I got him!"

HOME

At the end of the 2008 season I sat in a seat in the loge level of Shea Stadium, a couple of weeks before the last game was played there. The shell of as-yet-incomplete Citi Field loomed over the wall in right, being busily prepared to take over as the home of the Mets. A steady rain fell and the tarp hadn't been removed from the field. It was a Friday night. Our chances of seeing Johan Santana take on the Braves looked slimmer by the minute. From my seat beneath the overhanging upper deck I watched the videoboard where they were showing a montage of the team's 1986 run. The people around me, regulars, were rapt, absolutely fixated on the pixel-heavy images. It was all happening again. The Sox were up 5–3, Backman and Hernandez both flied out, and there were two down in the tenth, and we were watching it, the scattered thousands in the bright orange seats hoping to wait out the rain, we were watching it all over again.

A woman sat nearby, obviously a diehard, since the only humans left in rainy Queens that night were diehards, bored-looking ushers, and a tourist from Canada. The woman had on her Mets cap, a pencil behind her ear, and a scorecard close at hand. Maybe 40, she sat alone, and she watched the montage with unwavering attention.

Gary Carter singled. Kevin Mitchell came in to pinch hit for the pitcher, Rick Aguilera, and he singled, moving Carter to second. A buzz filled Shea, tarped and damp and mostly empty, and 22 years after the fact, but I swear to you the atmosphere began to change because the '86 Mets had two on the in the tenth and still had a breath left.

Ray Knight came up next, rapped a single up the middle that scored Carter. Applause. The Sox replaced Calvin Schiraldi with workhorse Bob Stanley, "The Steamer." Mookie Wilson stepped in for the Mets and the excitement among my rain-spattered peers rose palpably.

"Here it comes," I heard somebody say.

"Wow," I said under my breath, or so I'd thought. I gave a small, nervous chuckle.

"They show this, like, every delay," the woman said, turning to notice me. "It's always like this." Slight accent, maybe Long Island.

Then Bob Stanley lost his grip and his pitch sailed right toward Wilson, who danced awkwardly and was missed, and when the ball flew past Sox catcher Rich Gedman to the backstop Mitchell trotted in from third. The '86 Mets had tied it. More applause from people standing in the tunnels wearing rain ponchos, from the diehards. From me.

And so Mookie Wilson stepped in again. You can imagine how they were feeling in 1986 because maybe you've been fortunate enough to feel that way too. Their hearts were clenched. They stood because they couldn't sit, their nervous, twitching muscles wouldn't allow it. They wrung their hands, their caps. They wrung everything.

Oh God, Bob Stanley standing there on the mound in 1986, lank, perfectly still for the briefest moment. And then delivering the 3–2 pitch and Wilson smacking it up the first base line, a dribbler, really, a sad little hit.

Billy Buckner closed in on it. A hum rose in rainy Shea, all around me, a hum of recognition that increased in volume and intensity until we all saw it: E3 on your scorecard, maybe the most famous E3 of all time. The ball rolling through poor Buckner's legs. And Ray Knight stomping on home plate because the Mets had won, breaking all the hearts in New England.

A cheer went up—a cheer!—at Shea Stadium. The tarp remained in place, the seats sat almost completely empty, the rain fell. Nearby the jets roared in and out of LaGuardia. The puddles in Willets Point grew deeper, the rain filling them, the oil slicking atop them.

There were tears in the corners of my seat neighbour's eyes. She'd seen this a thousand times but it still moved her because the '86 Mets are what their fans whisper to themselves for consolation.

"Long time ago," I said to her.

"Yeah," she said. "Real long time ago." "Why the Mets?" I asked.

She said, "To most people the Mets' biggest crime is that they're not the Yankees. To us that's the best thing about them. They're ours."

"Do you have season tickets?" I asked.

"Yup, these are mine," she said, putting her arm over the seat next to her.

I told her I'd heard from another Mets fan that the team was making the move to the new park hard for some fans. Too expensive, fewer seats in that empty hulk out there beyond right field. All true, she said.

"You gonna make the move to Citi with them?" I asked. "Yeah," she said. "They're my team. You know."

And I do, as you do. You know because you, like me, have sat in your car, late for your shift and getting later, because your favourite play-by-play man is telling you that your team has runners on. So you sit in the edge of a parking lot while traffic slides by on the featureless commercial drive, and when your first baseman rips a double to the gap that scores two you pound the steering wheel and let out a whoop, knowing that whatever cold look or dressing down you're about to get from your manager will be worth it. You know it because, though your life seems to grow more confusing, not less, the act of watching, of cheering, is one that you understand better than most anything else. You know because it seems perfectly natural to find yourself in a strange bar somewhere making easy conversation with a stranger, with cold beer in brown glass bottles and the game on the TV over the bartender's head. You know because you've slid into seats in the upper deck, surrounded by thousands upon thousands of people you don't know and will never meet, and said to yourself: I'm home.

At rainy Shea we sat waiting for a game that wasn't going to be played. We knew that. We wouldn't see Santana pitch. We wouldn't even see him warm up. Not a single baseball appeared on the field, not one piece of equipment. But we stayed and talked baseball, and maybe the Mets fans thought to themselves, *At least they won't break my heart tonight.* And only once the loudspeakers rang with the news that the game had been officially called did we decamp, reluctantly, and make our way toward the trains, to home or a hotel room or a bar.

Here's the truth of it: the game makes sense. Down there on the field we know just what's at stake. It's a cleaner, truer expression of ourselves. It's something to make the hair on our arms stand up, something to hold dear and pass along and worry over. But here's the rest of that truth: it promises more torment and frustration than most of us would otherwise willingly invite into our lives. It requires loss and pain and heartbreak. It's not easy, not if you're doing it right.

That woman sitting near me in Shea Stadium had known all of that since '86. Frustration more continual than many of us can imagine. Imagine what it must have felt like to get back to the Series in 2000 only to lose to their more handsome cousins, the Yankees. What a kick to the head.

It's that pain, decades of it, and the pure joy of the thing too, that had her teary, sitting at a rained out game in 2008. And I thought for a moment, *Why do we do this to ourselves? Why would anyone do this to themselves?* But then, only love can break your heart, and love's always a thing worth having.

REVIVING SUMMER

They file into clubhouses in Sarasota, Fort Myers, Clearwater, and Dunedin. They arrive in Glendale, Peoria, Tucson, Mesa, and Goodyear. They fill lockers with their personal effects, they talk, joke, laugh. They stretch and jog, chew gum, play long toss. They begin to prepare for the long season ahead.

Summer is revived down there in Florida and Arizona. It's the preparation that makes possible games on the radio, peanuts, cold beer, your feet propped up on the bleacher row in front of you, short sleeves on hot afternoons, and inky-warm evenings. Look at them as a sort of vanguard, these ballplayers, an advance unit sent in to confirm for us the continued existence of sun and warmth. They tuck it in their back pockets and they promise to return it to us.

I love winter. Or maybe, as a Canadian, I've simply made my peace with it, been conditioned to endure the ceaseless parade of the seasons. Either way, once the Series wraps up in the fall, I begin looking forward to snow, to Nordic skiing and sledding with my kids, to sweaters, boots, and parkas. To life made smaller, gathered tight around the hearth. But there's no denying that a true northern winter takes a very real psychological toll. There comes a point when a person wants to be able to walk out the door without outfitting themselves against the possibility of death by freezing. And by the time that desire becomes most frenzied and desperate, along it comes:

"Pitchers and catchers report."

Few phrases elicit such joy, spark such hope. In the midst of so much slush and ice it's a reminder of all those summer things. Men who scattered across the globe at season's end begin to reassemble in clubhouses, to start again the pursuit of a championship, a campaign to be waged across the long summer ahead. The phenomenon is a perfectly timed salve to the winter-tortured mind.

It doesn't come in springtime here, of course. Far from it. February in Ontario is about as far from spring, let alone summer, as is possible—psychologically, meteorologically. But to be reminded, via Spring Training, that summer even exists is to be rescued. Summer, like a lifesaver, dropped alongside us where we flounder, that we may latch onto it and so be saved.

We all have our own notions of summer, memories, usually cherished seasons of sun that we hold onto and worry and long for to the point of desperation. Mine involve ball games. Live, on TV, over the radio. Specifically, I think about driving west with my wife years ago in a '94 Saturn, and about a night spent in a motel in Great Falls, Montana. We had just returned to the room from a game at Legion Park where the hometown Dodgers beat Missoula in dramatic fashion. The night was warm and there was a six-pack of beer on the nightstand. *Baseball Tonight* was on the TV and we had only a vague idea of the next day's destination. We'd been to a major league game in Milwaukee a few days before and would arrive at Safeco Field in Seattle a few days later, with a visit to Spokane's ballpark in between for good measure. As I cracked a beer I asked myself: *Is it possible to be happier?* And my conventional heart answered: *Not likely.*

Baseball offers escape of a sort, which we could all use now and then. My life is—knock wood—blessedly free of trauma and relatively devoid of obstacles, but that doesn't discount what Don DeLillo calls "the usual terror," the grind and assault of the day to day, the stresses, the emotional injuries. My anxiety makes me particularly adept at turning a negligible grain of trouble into a spectacular oyster of fear and regret. I lie awake at night for any number of reasons. They might differ from yours only in the specificity of their details. I worry about what I've done. I worry about what I haven't done. I worry about my children. I worry about death.

Baseball won't stave off death. I know this. It won't solve our myriad problems. Not mine, not yours, and not the world's. But the flash of hope I get from the phrase "pitchers and catchers report" feels like jumpstarting a car. It's a dark curtain peeled back. It sounds the way fresh-cut grass smells. If, as I suspect, the only way to confront death is to take pleasure in how we decorate the days beforehand, then I take extreme pleasure in those words, their sonority and cadence—pitchers and catchers report —and the hope they represent. Summer, warmth, colour.

Reliable as tides, regular as change, Spring Training is a marker of seasons, a reminder that time marches on, but its repetitive imposition of order also allows us to make some sense of the world. And in remembering the hope we had for our team last spring, and the one before that, we're reminded that narrative tends to swerve to avoid tidy summation. Making it through life's gauntlet intact requires both steadiness and, to nullify the drudgery, some things we can't know ahead of time. Winter promises spring, spring promises summer, and summer promises baseball; baseball promises surprises but doesn't tip its hand. That's what the opening of Spring Training offers: the cycle begun anew alongside the mystery of the potential ending. It offers hope.

I won't forget the things that worry me, those nettles that keep me up nights. But I'll temper them with summer memories, both dusty ones and those I've yet to create. And I'll give thanks to the men who offer me this sun-kissed distraction, these February missives from the green fields of Florida and Arizona. They, and the position players who'll follow them into camp, serve a spiritual purpose, as vessels of hope and dreaming. They're messengers, these ballplayers, the embodiment of cyclical change. When they break camp and come north, they'll bring summer with them.

162

Game number 162, for most teams and most fans, marks
the end of the season. Ten teams continue playing and tie
their fans' innards in knots until a Series champion emerges.
But for the majority of us the end of the regular season
is the end of direct involvement. The stadiums we have
frequented since April are padlocked and powered down.
Snow will pile up against some of them, and diamonds will
blur into indistinctness over the course of an off-season of
reasonable neglect.

Summer then becomes a thing to be tucked into the
camphor wood chest brought back from Shanghai, stashed
amid mothballs and yellowed photos, bronzed baby shoes,
silverware wrapped in an old kilt. Or it's a thing to be
deep-browsed on Instagram months from now, to marvel
at how long ago it already seems even without the bespoke
washing-out of a digital retro filter. Those hot days sliding
into benevolent evenings. Those games, all those games,
over now. It only makes sense that it would end like this. It
always does. And yet there's still this feeling.

Eighty-one times they threw open the gates and turnstiles
of each ballpark. Eighty-one afternoons and evenings they
tapped kegs and cooked up dogs and hawked popcorn. The
teams emerged from the dugout and stood for the anthem.
The players put their caps back on and the home team took
their positions on the field. Every team did these things,

the good ones and the bad ones. They all played eighty-one home games and another eighty-one on the road. How many of them do any of us remember?

In April, in May, the whole summer was laid out before us, endless and bottomless, a warm, rich thing full of colour and life. Those 162 games might as well have been a thousand. Every team was a contender. Your team, my team, could bolt from the gate. Maybe Opening Day would launch a momentous campaign that would shock prognosticators and even the most optimistic partisans, a season that would see records fall and the division won by August. When the weather is still cold, every season looks like a dream season.

The pitcher brought in over the winter would win 25 games and earn himself a Cy Young, or it would be that raggedy could-be ace suddenly emerging fully into something beyond even his perceived capacities. The new shortstop was a likely MVP, the aging third baseman still fielded at a Gold Glove level. The young players would mature quickly, the old ones age slowly. The stands would be full. It would not be like last year. It would not be like any year prior, except for the last year when things were great, when it all went right.

But the team was lousy. Or not lousy, not quite, but not good enough. The bats took ages to heat up, then froze with runners in scoring position. The rotation never found its groove. The bullpen was a bullpen, spotty and inconstant. Injuries, slumps. It was obvious at a certain point—by June? by the break?—that this team was not a contender, which left the better part of the season for enjoying baseball as baseball, innocent of consequence or even notional import. There were good games and terrible ones. The ritual act of watching and cheering. Each game stood as its own individual story, a bit of thumbnail theater on the theme of competition, effectively divorced from the standings.

It was a long season—they all are—and truthfully there were hard stretches, as losses mounted and the suspicion of futility became progressively more certain, but this is a different thing than being prepared for it to end. The end means the end of deciding on a whim to head down to the ballpark because the afternoon turned lovely and bright and there were tickets to be had. It silences the chance of a meaningless game on the radio, chattering away comfortingly in the background while work happens, or cleaning, or baking, or dozing off, or some other ordinary thing. Favourite players will not be there after having been there for months. They won't even be in town. They'll clear out their lockers and scatter to warmer locales. They might play golf or winter ball or disappear altogether into Florida or Arizona or some other temperate spot until spring.

This all happens every year, of course, but there is still a terrible poignancy to that last out, whatever the final score. The game is over. The season is over. There is drama to come in the playoff elimination games, and World Series heroics, the half-guilty choice of an October favourite or two. Still, the last insignificant game of baseball has been played this season, and so there is bereavement because the season is done and gone, and so by extension is the summer and all those things we'd meant to do or appreciate, all the opportunities we swore to take and didn't.

But here's where it's necessary to pan back, shelter in context, take the long view. We put our passions on a game that stretches back nearly a century and a half, which leaves so many seasons that have ended in frustration for all those forgotten teams, their fans dazed and disappointed.

But they have all come back. They have always come back. Scant months later those players congregated again and suited up and began once more the process of training and playing and losing and winning.

Another season will begin. And when it does, your team will again be a contender. So mourn the season, sure. Feel terrible. Thrash and mope and wail. Bury your cap and your jersey at the back of the closet, bemoan winter. This is okay. But know that you will be ready to love it again next season, and the season after that. Nothing is really finished. Recognize that you aren't done with baseball, because baseball is never really done. Spring always comes.